A Portraiture of Q (Volume 3); Taken fr the Education and 1 Social Manners, Civil a ̠ ̠ ̠litical Economy, Religious Principles and Character, of the Society of Friends

Thomas Clarkson

Alpha Editions

This edition published in 2024

ISBN 9789361477898

Design and Setting By

Alpha Editions

www.alphaedis.com

Email - info@alphaedis.com

Contents

CHAP. I.

Civil government—First tenet is, that governors have no right to interfere with the governed on the subject of Religion—and that if they interfere, and insist upon things which the conscience disapproves, the governed ought to refuse a compliance with them, and to bear patiently all the penalties annexed to such a refusal, but never to resist the governors by violence on this or any other account.

The Quakers hold four principles, which I shall distinguish by the name of Great Tenets. These are considered as arising out of the implied or positive injunctions of Christianity, and were insisted upon as essentials on the formation of the society. The first of these is on the subject of Civil Government.

Civil Government had existed long before the appearance of Christianity in the world. Legislators since that era, as they have imbibed its spirit, so they have introduced this spirit more or less into their respective codes. But, no nation has ever professed to change its system of jurisprudence, or to model it anew, in consequence of the new light which Christianity has afforded: neither have the alterations been so numerous in any nation, however high its profession of Christianity, with respect to laws, as to enable us to say, that there is any government in the known world, of Christian origin, or any government wholly upon the principles of the gospel.

If all men were to become real Christians, civil government would become less necessary. As there would be then no offences, there would be no need of magistracy or of punishment. As men would then settle any differences between them amicably, there would be no necessity for courts of law. As they would then never fight, there would be no need of armies. As they would then consider their fellow-creatures as brethren, they would relieve them as such, and there would be no occasion of laws for the poor. As men would then have more solicitude for the public good, and more large and liberal notions, than at any former time, they would of themselves conceive and raise all necessary public institutions and works. Government then is not so necessary for real Christians. It is necessary principally, as the apostle says, for evil-doers. But if it be chiefly necessary for evil-doers, then governors ought to be careful how they make laws, which may vex, harrass, and embarrass Christians, whom they will always find to be the best part of their communities, or, in other words, how they make laws, which Christians, on account of their religious scruples, cannot conscientiously obey.

It is a tenet of the Quakers, on the subject of government, that the civil magistrate has no right to interfere in religious matters, so as either to force any particular doctrines upon men, or to hinder them from worshipping God in their own way, provided that, by their creeds and worship, they do no detriment to others. The Quakers believe, however, that Christian churches may admonish such members as fall into error, and may even cut them off from membership, but this must be done not by the temporal, but by the spiritual sword.

This tenet the Quakers support, first, by reason. Religion, they say, is a matter solely, between God and man, that is, between God and that man who worships him. This must be obvious, they conceive, because man is not accountable to man for his religious opinions, except he binds himself to the discipline of any religious society, but to God alone. It must be obvious again, they say, because no man can be a judge over the conscience of another. He can know nothing of the sincerity or hypocrisy of his heart. He can be neither an infallible judge, nor an infallible correcter of his religious errors. "The conscience of man, says Barclay, is the seat and throne of God in him, of which he alone is the proper and infallible judge, who, by his power and spirit, can rectify its mistakes." It must be obvious again, they say, from the consideration that, if it were even possible for one man to discern the conscience of another, it is impossible for him to bend or controul it. But conscience is placed both out of his sight and of his reach. It is neither visible nor tangible. It is inaccessible by stripes or torments. Thus, while the body is in bondage, on account of the religion of the soul, the soul itself is free, and, while it suffers under torture, it enjoys the divinity, and feels felicity in his presence. But if all these things are so, it cannot be within the province either of individual magistrates or of governments, consisting of fallible men, to fetter the consciences of those who may live under them. And any attempt to this end is considered by the Quakers as a direct usurpation of the prerogative of God.

This tenet the Quakers adopt again on a contemplation of the conduct and doctrines of Jesus Christ and of his apostles. They find nothing in these, which can give the least handle to any man to use force in the religious concerns of another. During the life of Jesus Christ upon earth, it is no where recorded of him, that he censured any man for his religion. It is true that he reproved the Scribes and Pharisees, but this was on account of their hypocrisy, because they pretended to be what they were not. But he no where condemned the devout Jew, who was sincere in his faith. But if he be found no where to have censured another for a difference in religious opinions, much less was it ever said of him, that he forced him to the adoption of his own. In the memorable instance, where James and John were willing to have called fire from Heaven, to burn those who refused to receive him, he rebuked them by an assurance, that "they knew not what spirit they were of." And, with respect to his doctrines, nothing can be more full to the point than his saying, that "his kingdom was not of this world," by which he meant that his dominion was wholly of a spiritual nature, and that men must cast off all worldly imaginations, and become spiritually minded, before, they could belong to him. But no application of outward force, in the opinion of the Quakers, can thus alter the internal man. Nor can even the creeds and doctrines of others produce this effect, except they become sanctioned by the divine influence on the heart.

Neither is it recorded of any of the apostles, that they used any other weapons than those of persuasion and the power of God in the propagation of their doctrines, leaving such as did not choose to follow them to their own way. They were explicit also in stating the spiritual nature of Christ's kingdom, from whence an inference similar to the former is deducible, namely, that no compulsory interference can be effectual in matters of religion. And St. Paul, in particular, tells the Corinthians, that, in his spiritual services to them, he does not consider himself "as having any dominion over their faith, but as helpers of their joy."

[Footnote 1: 2 Cor. i. 24.]

But if neither Jesus Christ, who was the author of that religion, which many civil governments have established, nor the apostles, who afterwards propagated it, forced their doctrines upon other men, or hindered them by force from worshipping in their own way, even though the former could have called legions of angels to his support, it certainly does not become weak, ignorant, and fallible men, because they are placed in the situation of governors, to set up their own creeds as supreme, and to throw penalties and restrictions in the way of the religious exercise of others.

But if governors, contrary to the example of Jesus Christ and of his apostles, should interfere in religious matters, and impose laws upon the governed, of which, as Christians, they cannot but disapprove, then the Quakers are of opinion, that the governed ought always to obey the laws of Jesus Christ, rather than the laws of any governors, who are only men. Thus when Peter and John were commanded by the rulers of the Jews to speak no more in the name of Jesus, they dared not yield obedience to their commands, reasoning thus, "Whether it be right in the sight of God to hearken unto you more than unto God, judge ye."

[Footnote 2: Acts iv. 19.]

And as the governed in such case ought, in obedience to God, the Supreme Ruler of the Universe, and the King of Kings, to refuse a compliance with the laws of their own governors, so they ought to be prepared patiently to submit to the penalties which are annexed to such refusal, and on no account, if just representations made in the meek and quiet spirit of their religion, are not likely to be effectual, to take up arms or resist them by force. And this doctrine they ground, first, on the principle, that it is not only more noble, but more consistent with their duty as Christians, to suffer, than to give growth to the passions of revenge, or by open resistance to become the occasion of loss of life to others. And, secondly, on the example of Jesus Christ, and of the apostles and primitive Christians, all of whom patiently submitted to the pains and penalties inflicted upon them by the governments of their respective times for the exercise of their religion.

CHAP. II.

Oaths—Quakers conceive it unlawful for Christians to take an oath—their sufferings on this account—Consider oaths as unnecessary—as having an immoral tendency, which even the Heathens allowed—and as having been forbidden by Jesus Christ—Explanation of the scriptural passages cited on this occasion—Christianity not so perfect with the lawfulness of oaths as without it—Other reasons taken from considerations relative to the ancient oath "by the name of God"

A second tenet, which the Quakers hold, is, that it is unlawful for Christians to take a civil oath.

Many and grievous were the sufferings of the Quakers, in the early part of their history, on account of their refusing to swear before the civil magistrate. They were insulted, fined, and imprisoned. Some of the judges too indulged a rancour against them on this account, unworthy of their high office, which prescribed justice impartially to all. For when they could not convict them of the offences laid to their charge, they administered to them the oath of allegiance, knowing that they would not take it, and that confiscation of property and imprisonment would ensue. But neither ill usage, nor imprisonment, nor loss of property, ever made any impression upon the Quakers, so as to induce them to swear in judicial cases, and they continued to suffer, till the legislature, tired out with the cries of their oppression, decreed, that their affirmation should in all cases except criminal, or in that of serving upon juries, or in that of qualifications for posts of honour or emolument under government, be received as equivalent to their oath. And this indulgence towards them is continued to them by law to the present day.

The Quakers have an objection to oaths, as solemn appeals to God, because they are unnecessary.

It is an old saying among the Quaker writers, that "truth was before all oaths." By this they mean, there was a time, when men's words were received as truths, without the intervention of an oath. Ancient fable, indeed, tells us, that there were no oaths in the golden age, but that, when men departed from their primitive simplicity, and began to quarrel with one another, they had recourse to falsehood to substantiate their own case, after which it became necessary, that some expedient should be devised, in the case of disputes, for the ascertaining the truth. Hence Hesiod makes the god of oaths the son of Esis or of contention. This, account differs but little from that of Polybuis, who says, that the use of oaths in judgment was rare among the ancients, but that, as perfidy grew, oaths increased.

And as it is a saying of the Quakers, that "truth was before all oaths," so they believe, that truth would be spoken, if oaths were done away. Thus, that which is called honour by the world, will bind men to the truth, who perhaps know but little of religion. But if so, then he, who makes Christianity his guide, will not be found knowingly in a falsehood, though he be deprived of the opportunity of swearing.

But if it be true, that truth existed before the invention of oaths, and that truth would still be spoken, even if all oaths were abolished, then the Quakers say, that oaths are not so necessary as some have imagined, because they have but a secondary effect in the production of the truth. This conclusion they consider also as the result of reason. For good men will speak truth without an oath, and bad men will hardly be influenced by one. And where oaths are regarded, it is probable that truth is forced out of men, not so much, because they consider them as solemn appeals to God, as that they consider the penalties, which will follow their violation; so that a simple affirmation, under the same pains and penalties, would be equally productive of the truth.

The Quakers consider oaths again as very injurious to morality. For first, they conceive it to be great presumption in men to summon God as a witness in their trilling and earthly concerns.

They believe, secondly, that, if men accustom themselves to call upon God on civil occasions, they render his name so familiar to them, that they are likely to lose the reverence due to it, or so to blend religious with secular considerations, that they become in danger of losing sight of the dignity, solemnity, and awfulness of devotion. And it is not an unusual remark, that persons, most accustomed to oaths, are the most likely to perjury. A custom-house oath has become proverbial in our own country. I do not mean by this to accuse mercantile men in particular, but to state it as a received opinion, that, where men make solemn things familiar, there is a danger of their moral degradation. Hence the Quakers consider the common administration of oaths to have a tendency that is injurious to the moral interests of men.

This notion relative to the bad tendency of oaths, the Quakers state to have prevailed even in the Gentile world. As Heathen philosophy became pure, it branded the system of swearing as pernicious to morals. It was the practice of the Persians to give each other their right hand as a token of their speaking the truth. He, who gave his hand deceitfully, was accounted more detestable than if he had sworn the Scythians, in their conference with Alexander the Great, addressed him thus: "Think not that the Scythians confirm their friendship by an oath. They swear by keeping their word." The Phrygians were wholly against oaths. They neither took them themselves, nor required them of others. Among the proverbs of the Arabs, this was a celebrated one, "Never swear, but let thy word be yes or no." So religious was Hercules, says Plutarch, that he never swore but once. Clinias, a Greek philosopher, and a scholar of Pythagoras, is said to have dreaded an oath so much, that, when by swearing he could have escaped a fine of three talents, he chose rather to pay the money than do it, though he was to have sworn nothing but the truth. Indeed, throughout all Greece, the system of swearing was considered as of the most immoral tendency, the very word, which signified "perjured," in the Greek language, meaning, when analysed, "he that adds oath to oath," or "the taker of many oaths."

But, above all, the Quakers consider oaths as unlawful for Christians, having been positively forbidden by Jesus Christ.

The words, in which they conceived this prohibition to have been contained, they take from the sermon on the Mount.

"Again, ye have heard, that it hath been said by them of old time, Thou shalt not forswear thyself, but shall perform unto the Lord thine oaths."

[Footnote 3: Matt. v. 33.]

"But I say unto you, swear not at all, neither by heaven, because it is God's throne."

"Nor by the earth, for it is his footstool: neither by Jerusalem, for it is the city of the great King."

"Neither shalt thou swear by thy head, because thou canst not make one hair white or black."

"But let your communication be yea, yea; nay, nay: for whatsoever is more than this cometh of evil."

It is said by those, who oppose the Quakers on this subject, that these words relate, not to civil oaths, but to such as are used by profane persons in the course of their conversation. But the Quakers deny this, because the disciples, as Jews, must have known that profane swearing had been unlawful long before this prohibition of Jesus Christ. They must relate, therefore, to something else, and to something, which had not before been forbidden.

They deny it also on account of the construction of the sentences, and of the meaning of the several words in these. For the words, "Swear not at all," in the second of the verses, which have been quoted, have an immediate reference to the words in the first. Thus they relate to the word "forswear," in the first. But if they relate to the word "forswear," they must relate to perjury, and if to perjury, then to a civil oath, or to an oath, where an appeal is made to God by man, as to something relating to himself. The word oath also is explicitly mentioned in the first of these verses, and mentioned as an oath which had been allowed. Now there was one oath, which had been allowed in ancient time. The Jews had been permitted, in matters of judgment, to swear by the name of God. This permission was given them, for one, among other reasons, that they might be prevented from swearing by the name of those idols by which their neighbours swore; for a solemn appeal to any Heathen god necessarily includes an acknowledgment of the omnipresence of the same.

That they related to this oath in particular, the Quakers conceive to be obvious from the prohibition in the verses which have been cited, of swearing by heaven, by earth, and by other things. The Jews, knowing the sacredness of the name of God, had an awful notion of the consequences of perjury, if committed after an appeal to it, and therefore had recourse to the names of the creatures, in case they should swear falsely. But even the oaths, thus substituted by them, are forbidden by Jesus Christ; and they are forbidden upon this principle, as we find by a subsequent explanation given by St. Matthew, that whosoever swore by these creatures, really and positively swore by the name of God. But if they are forbidden, because swearing by these creatures is the same thing as swearing by God who made them, then the oath "by the name of God," which had been permitted to the Jews of old, was intended by Jesus Christ to be discontinued, or to have no place in his new religion.

The Quakers then, considering the words in question to have the meaning now annexed to them, give the following larger explanation of what was the intention of our Saviour upon this occasion.

In his sermon on the Mount, of which these words on the subject of oaths are a part, he inculcated into his disciples a system of morality, far exceeding that of the Jews, and therefore in the verses which precede those upon this subject, he tells them, that whereas it was said of old, "thou shall not kill," he expected of them, that they should not even entertain the passion of revenge. And whereas it was said of old, "thou shalt not commit adultery," he expected, that they should not even lust after others, if they were married, or after those in a married state. Thus he brings both murder and adultery from act to thought. He attaches a criminality to unlawful feelings if not suppressed, or aims at the subjugation of the passions, as the springs of the evil actions of men. Going on to shew the farther superiority of his system of morality over that of the Jews, he says again, whereas it was said of old, "thou shall not forswear thyself," he expects that they should not swear at all, not even by the name of God, which had been formerly allowed, for that he came to abrogate the ancient law, and perjury with it. It was his object to make the word of his true disciples equal to the ancient oath. Thus he substituted truth for oaths. And he made this essential difference between a Jew and a Christian, that, whereas the one swore in order that he might be believed; the other was to speak truth in order that he might not swear. Such was the intended advance from Jew to Christian, or from Moses to Christ.

The Quakers are farther confirmed in their ideas upon this subject, by believing, that Christianity would not have been as perfect as they apprehend it to have been intended to be, without this restriction upon oaths. Is it possible, they say, that Jesus Christ would have left it to Christians to imagine, that their words were to be doubted on any occasion? Would he have left it to them to think so dishonourably of one another, or of their new vocation, that their words were to be tried by the touchstone of oaths, when his religion was to have a greater effect than any former system of morality ever known, in the production of truth? Is it possible, when oaths sprung out of fraud and falsehood, as he himself witnesses, (for whatever is more than yea and nay, cometh of evil) that he would have left this remnant of antiquity standing, as if his religion was not intended to extirpate the very ground-work of it?

Finally, the Quakers are confirmed in their ideas upon this subject from a belief that oaths were to cease, either at the coming of Jesus Christ, or as men became Christians. For, in the first place, the oath "by the name of God," is considered by some, as I have before noticed, to have been permitted to the Jews during their weak state, that they might not swear by the idols of their cotemporary neighbours, and thus lose sight of the only and true God. But what Christian stands in need of any preservative against idolatry, or of any commemorative of the existence and superintendence of an almighty, wise, beneficent, and moral Governor of the world? Some again have imagined, that, as the different purifications among the Jews, denoting the holiness of God, signified that it became men to endeavour to be holy, so the oath "by the name of God," denoting the verity of God, signified, that it became men to devote themselves to the truth. But no true Christian stands in need of such symbols, to make him consider his word as equivalent to his oath. Others again have imagined, that the oath "by the name of God," typified the truth, or the eternal word. But as the type ceases when the antitype appears, so the coming of Jesus Christ, who in the gospel language is called both the truth and the eternal word, may be considered as putting an end to this, as to other types and shadows, of the Jewish church.

CHAP. III.

SECT. I.

War—Tenet on war—Quakers hold it unlawful for Christians to fight—Scriptural passages, which they produce in support of this tenet—Arguments which others produce from scriptural authority against it—Reply of the Quakers to these arguments.

The next of the great tenets which the Quakers hold, is on the subject of war. They believe it unlawful for Christians to engage in the profession of arms, or indeed to bear arms under any circumstances of hostility whatever. Hence there is no such character as that of a Quaker soldier. A Quaker is always able to avoid the regular army, because the circumstance of entering into it is a matter of choice. But where he has no such choice, as is the case in the militia, he either submits, if he has property, to distraints upon it, or, if he has not, to prison.

[Footnote 4: The Quakers have been charged with inconsistency in refusing military service, and yet in paying those taxes, which are expressly for the support of wars. To this charge they reply, that they believe it to be their duty to render to Caesar the things which are Caesar's, and to leave the application of them to Caesar himself, as he judges best for the support of government. This duty they collect from the example of Jesus Christ, who paid the tribute money himself, and ordered his disciples to do it, and this to a government, not only professedly military, but distinguished for its idolatry and despotism. Personal service, however, they conceive to militate against a positive command by our Saviour, as will be explained in this chapter.]

The Quakers ground the illicitness of war on several passages, which are to be found in the New Testament. I shall not quote all the texts they bring forward, but shall make a selection of them on this occasion.

Jesus Christ, in the famous sermon, which he preached upon the Mount, took occasion to mention specifically some of the precepts of the Jewish law, and to inform his hearers, that he expected of those, who were to be his true disciples, that they would carry these to a much higher extent in their practice under the new dispensation, which he was then affording them. Christianity required a greater perfection of the human character than under the law. Men were not only not to kill, but not even to cherish the passion of revenge. And "whereas it was said of old, an eye for an eye, and a tooth for a tooth, I say unto you, says Christ, that ye resist not evil; but whosoever shall smite thee on thy right cheek, turn to him the other also."

And farther on in the same chapter, he says, "Ye have heard that it hath been said, Thou shalt love thy neighbour, and hate thine enemy: But I say unto you, love your enemies, bless them that curse you, do good to them that hate you, and pray for them that despitefully use you and persecute you. For if ye love them which love you, what reward have you? do not even the Publicans the same? Be ye therefore perfect, even as your Father which is in heaven is perfect." Now the Quakers are of opinion, that no man can receive this doctrine his heart, and assist either offensively or defensively in the operations of war.

[Footnote 5: Matt. v. 38.]

[Footnote 6: The Heathen nations, on account of their idolatry, were called enemies by the Jews.]

Other passages, quoted by the Quakers, in favour of their tenet on war, are taken from the apostles Paul and James conjointly.

The former, in his second epistle to the Corinthians, says, "For though we walk in the flesh, we do not war after the flesh: For the weapons of our warfare are not carnal, but mighty through God to the pulling down of strong holds, to the casting down imaginations, and every high thing that exalteth itself against the knowledge of God, and bringing into captivity every thought to the obedience of Christ." From hence the Quakers argue, that the warfare of Christianity, or that which Christianity recognises, is not carnal, but spiritual, and that it consists in the destruction of the evil imaginations, or of the evil lusts and passions of men. That is, no man can be a true soldier of Christ, unless his lusts are subdued, or unless the carnal be done away by the spiritual mind. Now this position having been laid down by St. Paul, or the position having been established in Christian morals, that a state of subjugated passions is one of the great characteristic marks of a true Christian, the Quakers draw a conclusion from it by the help of the words of St. James. This apostle, in his letter to the dispersed tribes, which were often at war with each other, as well as with the Romans, says, "From whence come wars and fightings among you? Come they not hence even of your lusts that war in your members?" But if wars come from the lusts of men, then the Quakers say, that those who have subdued their lusts, can no longer engage in them, or, in other words, that true Christians, being persons of this description, or being such, according to St. Paul, as are redeemed out of what St. James calls the very grounds and occasions of wars, can no longer fight. And as this proposition is true in itself, so the Quakers conceive the converse of it to be true also: For if there are persons, on the other hand, who deliberately engage in the wars and fightings of the world, it is a proof, that their lusts are not yet subjugated, or that, though they may be nominal, they are not yet arrived at the stature of true or of full-grown Christians.

[Footnote 7: 2 Cor. x. 3, 4, 5.]

[Footnote 8: James iv. I.]

A third quotation, made by the Quakers, is taken from St. Paul exclusively. "Now if any man have not the spirit of Christ, he is none of his." That is, if men have not the same disposition which Jesus Christ manifested in the different situations of his life, the same spirit of humility and of forbearance, and of love, and of forgiveness of injuries, or if they do not follow him as a pattern, or if they do not act as he would have done on any similar occasion, they are not Christians. Now they conceive, knowing what the spirit of Jesus was by those things which have been recorded of him, that he could never have been induced or compelled, by any earthly consideration or power, to have engaged in the wars of the world. They are aware that his mission, which it became him to fulfil, and which engrossed all his time, would not have allowed him the opportunity of a military life. But they believe, independently of this, that the spirit which he manifested upon earth, would have been of itself a sufficient bar to such an employment. This they judge from his opinions and his precepts. For how could he have taken up arms to fight, who enjoined in the new dispensation, that men were not to resist evil; that they were to love their enemies; that they were to bless those who cursed them, and to do good to those who hated them? This they judge also from his practice. For how could he have lifted up his arm against another, who, "when he was reviled, reviled not again;" and who, in his very agony upon the Cross, prayed for his persecutors, saying, "Father, forgive them, for they know not what they do." But if Jesus Christ could not have been induced or compelled to have engaged in a profession, which would have subjected him to take away the life of another, so neither can any Christian; "for if a man have not the spirit of Christ, he is none of his."

[Footnote 9: Rom. viii. 9.]

Three arguments are usually brought against the Quakers on this subject.

The first is, that John the Baptist, when the soldiers demanded of him what they should do, did not desire them to leave the service in which they were engaged, but, on the other hand, to be content with their wages. To this the Quakers reply, that John told them also, "to do violence to no man." But even if he had not said this, they apprehend that nothing could be deduced from his expressions, which could become binding upon Christians. For John was the last prophet of the old dispensation, but was never admitted into the new. He belonged to the system which required an eye for an eye, and a tooth for a tooth, but not to that which required no resistance to evil, and which insisted upon the love of enemies as well as of friends. Hence Jesus Christ said of him, that "he who was least in the kingdom of heaven, was greater than he."

[Footnote 10: Luke iii. 14.]

The second argument brought against the Quakers on this occasion, is of a similar nature with the former. It is said that, if war had been unlawful, our Saviour, when the centurion came to him at Capernaum, would have found fault with his profession; but he did not do this, but on the other hand he highly commended him for his religion. In answer to this the Quakers observe, first, that no solid argument can be drawn from silence on any occasion. Secondly, that Jesus Christ seems, for wise purposes, to have abstained from meddling with many of the civil institutions of his time, though in themselves wicked, thinking probably, that it was sufficient to have left behind him such general precepts, as, when applied properly, would be subversive of them all. And, thirdly, that he never commended the centurion on account of his military situation, but on account of his profession of his faith.

[Footnote 11: Matt. viii. 5.]

They say farther, that they can bring an argument of a much more positive nature than that just mentioned, from an incident which took place, and where Jesus was again concerned. When Peter cut off the ear of one of the servants of the high priest, who was concerned in the apprehension of his Lord, he was not applauded, but reprimanded for the part which he thus took in his defence in the following words: "Put up again thy sword in its place, for all they that take the sword, shall perish by the sword." Now the Quakers conceive, that much more is to be inferred against the use of the sword from this instance, than from the former in favour of it.

[Footnote 12: Matt. xxvi, 52.]

The last argument, which is usually adduced against the Quakers on this subject, is, that they have mistaken the meaning of the words of the famous sermon upon the Mount. These words teach us the noble lesson, that it is more consistent with the character of a Christian to forgive, than to resist an injury. They are, it is said, wholly of private import, and relate solely to private occurrences in life. But the Quakers have extended the meaning of them beyond private to public injuries or wars.

The Quakers, in answer to this observe, that they dare not give to the words in question a less extensive meaning. They relate to every one who reads them. They relate to the poor. They relate to the rich. They relate to, every potentate who may be the ruler of a land. They relate to every individual of his council. There is no exception, or dispensation to any one, in favour of any case.

That they relate to public as well as private wars, or that they extend themselves naturally to those which are public, the Quakers conceive it reasonable to suppose from the following consideration. No man, they apprehend, can possess practically the divine principle of loving an individual enemy at home, or of doing good to the man who hates him, but he must of necessity love his enemy in any and every other place. He must have gone so for forward on the road to Christian perfection, as to be unable to bear arms against any other person whatsoever, and particularly when, according to the doctrines of the New Testament, no geographical boundaries fix the limits of love and enmity between man and man, but the whole human race are considered as the children of the same parent, and therefore as brothers to one another. But who can truly love an enemy and kill him? And where is the difference, under the Gospel dispensation, between Jew and Gentile, Greek and Barbarian, bond and free?

That these words were meant to extend to public as well as to private ware, the Quakers believe again from the views which they entertain relative to the completion of prophecy. They believe that a time will come, in one or other of the succeeding ages, "when men shall bent their swords into ploughshares, and their spears into pruning-hooks, and when nation shall not lift up sword against nation, and they shall not learn war any more." Now other Christians, who differ from them in the interpretation of the words in question, believe equally with them, that the times thus predicted will come to pass. The question then is, whether the more enlarged interpretation of these words, as insisted upon by the Quakers, or of the less enlarged as insisted upon by others, be the most consistent with the belief of the future accomplishment of the prophecy just mentioned. And in this case the Quakers are of opinion, that if wars were ever to cease, one ought to expect that some foundation would have been previously laid in Christianity for this great and important end. The subjugation of the passions, which it is the direct tendency of Christianity to effect, would produce this end. And so far such a foundation has already been laid in this system. But as the admission of moral precepts into the education of man, so as to form habits of moral opinion, is another, way of influencing conduct in life, the Quakers think it likely that some such maxim as "that Christians should not fight," would have been introduced also, because the adoption of such a maxim would have had a similar tendency with the subjugation of the passions in producing the same end. For it seems absurd, they conceive, to suppose that wars should cease, and that no precept should have been held out that they were wrong. But the more enlarged interpretation of the words in question furnishes such a precept, and therefore another foundation seems to have been laid in Christianity for the same end. They admit, therefore, the larger interpretation as included in the less, because it comports more with the design of Providence, who, by the mouth of his prophets wills universal peace, that the prohibition of public as well as of private wars should be understood as a Christian doctrine, than that the words in question should be confined to private injuries alone.

The last reason, which the Quakers give for adopting the larger interpretation of the words in the sermon upon the Mount, as well as the less, is the following. They are of opinion, that, as Christians, they ought not to lessen the number of the moral obligations of the Gospel. They ought not to abridge its dignity, nor to put limits to its benevolence. If it was the desire of Jesus Christ, that men should love their enemies, it is their duty to believe, that his wish could not have been otherwise than universal. If it was an object with him to cure moral evil, it is their duty to suppose, that it was his desire to destroy it, not partially, but to the utmost possible extent. If it was his design to give happiness to man, it is their duty to determine, that he intended to give it not in a limited proportion, but in the largest measure. But when they consider the nature of wars, that they militate against the law of preservation, that they include the commission of a multitude of crimes, that they produce a complication of misery and suffering to man, they conceive they would not be doing their duty as Christians, or giving to Christianity its due honour, if they were not to admit the larger meaning of the words in question as well as the less. Reason too, pleads for the one as well as for the other. Consistency of moral doctrine again demands both. But if we admit the restricted interpretation, and exclude the larger, we offend reason. All consistency is at an end. Individual responsibility for moral turpitude will be taken from man. Crimes, clearly marked and defined in the page of Christianity, will cease to be crimes at the will of princes. One contradiction will rush in after another; and men will have two different standards of morality, as they adhere to the commands of the Gospel, or to the customs of governments or of the world.

SECT. II.

_Meaning of the scriptural passages advanced by the Quakers, supported by the opinions and practice of the early Christians—Early Christian writers held it unlawful for Christians to fight, as appears from Justin—Tatian—Clemens—and others—Christians would not enter into the armies for more than two centuries, as appears from Ireneus—Tertullian —Celsus—Origen and others—and generally left the military service, if they happened to be converted in it.

It may be presumed to be difficult for Christians, who have been in the habit of seeing wars entered into and carried on by their own and other Christian governments, and without any other censure than that they might be politically wrong, to see the scriptural passages of "non-resistance to evil and love of enemies," but through a vitiated medium. The prejudices of some, the interests of others, and custom with all, will induce a belief among them, that these have no relation to public wars. At least they will be glad to screen themselves under such a notion. But the question is, what a Heathen would have said to these passages, who, on his conversion to Christianity, believed that the New Testament was of divine origin, that it was the book of life, and that the precepts, which it contained, were not to be dispensed with, to suit particular cases, without the imputation of evil. Now such a trial, the Quakers say, has been made. It was made by the first Christians, and they affirm, that these interpreted the passages, which have been mentioned, differently from those of most of the Christians of the present age; for that both their opinions and their practice spoke loudly against the lawfulness of war.

Upon this new subject I shall enter next. And I confess I shall enter upon it willingly. First, because I know of none that is more important. Secondly, because, though controversy may have thrown some light upon it, much remains to be added. And, thirdly, because the assertions of the Quakers on this point are disputed by many at the present day. With respect to the opinions of the early Quakers, which I shall notice first, it must be premised, that such of them as have written books, have not all of them entered on this subject. Some of them have not had even occasion to mention it. But where they have, and where they have expressed an opinion, I believe that this will be found unfavourable to the continuance of war.

Justin the Martyr, one of the earliest writers in the second century, considers war as unlawful. He makes also the devil "the author of all war." No severer sentence could have been passed upon it than this, when we consider it as coming from the lips of an early Christian. The sentiment too was contrary to the prevailing sentiments of the times, when, of all professions, that of war was most honourable, and was the only one that was considered to lead to glory. It resulted, therefore, in all probablity, from the new views, which Justin had acquired by a perusal of such of the scriptures, as had then fallen into his hands.

Tatian, who was the disciple of Justin, in his oration to the Greeks, speaks precisely in the same terms on the same subject.

From the different expressions of Clemens of Alexandria, a contemporary of the latter, we collect his opinion to be decisive against the lawfulness of war.

Tertullian, who may be mentioned next in order of time, strongly condemned the practice of bearing arms, as it related to Christians. I shall give one or two extracts from him on this subject. In his dissertation on the worship of idols, he says, "Though the soldiers came to John, and received a certain form to be observed, and though the centurion believed, yet Jesus Christ, by disarming Peter, disarmed every soldier afterwards: for custom never sanctions an illicit act." And in his "Soldier's Garland," he says, "Can a soldier's life be lawful, when Christ has pronounced, that he who lives by the sword shall perish by the sword? Can one, who professes the peaceable doctrines of the Gospel, be a soldier, when it is his duty not so much as to go to law? and shall he, who is not to revenge his own wrongs, be instrumental in bringing others into chains, imprisonment, torment, death?"

Cyprian, in his Epistle to Donatus, takes a view of such customs in his own times, as he conceived to be repugnant to the spirit or the letter of the Gospel. In looking at war, which was one of them, he speaks thus: "Suppose thyself, says he, with me on the top of some very exalted eminence, and from thence looking down upon the appearances of things beneath thee. Let our prospect take in the whole horizon, and let us view, with the indifference of persons not concerned in them, the various motions and agitations of human life. Thou wilt then, I dare say, have a real compassion for the circumstances of mankind, and for the posture in which this view will represent them. And when thou reflectest upon thy condition, thy thoughts will rise in transports of gratitude and praise to God for having made thy escape from the pollutions of the world. The things thou wilt principally observe, will be the highways beset with robbers, the seas with pirates, encampments, marches, and all the terrible forms of war and, bloodshed. When a single murder is committed, it shall be deemed perhaps a crime; but that crime shall commence a virtue, when committed under the shelter of public authority, so that punishment is not rated by the measure of guilt, but the more enormous the size of the wickedness is, so much the greater is the chance for impunity." These are the sentiments of Cyprian, and that they were the result of his views of Christianity, as taken from the divine writings, there can be little doubt. If he had stood upon the same eminence, and beheld the same sights previously to his conversion, he might, like others, have neither thought piracy dishonourable, nor war inglorious.

Lactantius, who lived some time after Cyprian, in his treatise "Concerning the True Worship of God," says, "It can never be lawful for a righteous man to go to war, whose warfare is in righteousness itself," And in another part of the same treatise he observes, that "no exception can be made with respect to this command of God. It can never be lawful to kill a man, whose person the Divine Being designed to be sacred as to violence."

It will be unnecessary to make extracts from other of the early Christian writers, who mention this subject. I shall therefore only observe, that the names of Origen, Archelaus, Ambrose, Chrysostom, Jerom, and Cyril, may be added, to those already mentioned, as the names of persons who gave it as their opinion, that it was unlawful for Christians to go to war.

With respect to the practice of the early Christians, which is the next point to be considered, it may be observed, that there is no well authenticated instance upon record, of Christians entering into the army for the first two centuries; but it is true, on the other hand, that they declined the military profession, as one in which it was not lawful for them to engage.

The first species of evidence, which I shall produce to this point, may be found in the following facts, which reach from the year 169 to the year 198, Avidius Crassus had rebelled against the emperor Verus, and was slain in a short time afterwards. Clodius Albinus in one part of the world, and Pescenninus Niger in another, rebelled against the emperor Severus, and both were slain likewise. Now suspicion fell, as it always did in these times, if any thing went wrong, upon the Christians, as having been concerned upon these occasions. But Tertullian, in his Discourse to Scapula, tells us, that no Christians were to be found in these armies. And yet these armies were extensive. Crassus was master of all Syria, with its four legions, Niger of the Asiatic and Egyptian legions, and Albinus of those of Britain, which legions together contained between a third and an half of the standing legions of Rome. And the fact, that no Christians were to be found in these, is the more remarkable, because, according to the same Tertullian, Christianity had reached all the places, in which these armies were.

A second species of evidence, as far as it goes, may be collected from expressions and declarations in the works of certain authors of those times. Justin the Martyr, and Tatian, make distinctions between soldiers and Christians; and the latter says, that the Christians declined even military commands. Clemens of Alexandria, gives the Christians, who were cotemporary with him, the appellation of "peaceable, or of the followers of peace," thus distinguishing them from the soldiers of his age. And he says expressly, that "those, who were the followers of peace, used none of the instruments of war."

A third species of evidence, which is of the highest importance in this case, is the belief which the writers of these times had, that the prophecy of Isaiah, which stated, that men should turn their swords into ploughshares, and their spears into pruning-hooks, was then in the act of completion.

Irenæus, who flourished about the year 180, affirms, that this famous prophecy had been completed in his time; "for the Christians, says he, have changed their swords and their lances into instruments of peace, and they know not how to fight," Justin Martyr, who was cotemporary with Irenæus, asserted the same thing, which he could not have done if the Christians in his time had engaged in war. "That the prophecy, says he, is fulfilled, you have good reason to believe, for we, who in times past killed one another, do not now fight with our enemies." And here it is observable, that the word "fight" does not mean to strike, or to beat, or to give a blow, but to fight as in war; and the word "enemy" does not mean a common adversary, or one who has injured us, but an enemy of the state; and the sentence, which follows that which has been given, puts the matter again out of all doubt. Tertullian, who lived after these, speaks in those remarkable words: "Deny that these (meaning the turning of swords into ploughshares) are the things prophesied of, when you see what you see, or that they are the things fulfilled, when you read what you read; but if you deny neither of these positions, then you must confess, that the prophecy has been accomplished, as far as the practice of every individual is concerned, to whom it is applicable." I might go from Tertullian even as far as Theoderet, if it were necessary, to shew, that the prophecy in question was considered as in the act of completion in those times.

The fourth and last proof will be found in the assertions of Celsus, and in the reply of Origen to that writer. Celsus, who lived at the end of the second century, attacked the Christian religion. He made it one of his charges against the Christians, that they refused in his time to bear arms for the emperor, even in the case of necessity, and when their services would have been accepted. He told them farther, that if the rest of the empire were of their opinion, it would soon be overrun by the Barbarians. Now Celsus dared not have brought this charge against the Christians, if the fact had not been publicly known. But let us see whether it was denied by those, who were of opinion that his work demanded a reply. The person, who wrote against him in favour of Christianity, was Origen, who lived in the third century. But Origen, in his answer, admits the fact as stated by Celsus, that the Christians would not bear arms, and justifies them for refusing the practice on the principle of the unlawfulness of war.

And as the early Christians would not enter into the armies, so there is good ground to suppose, that, when they became converted in them, they relinquished their profession. Human nature was the same both in and out of the armies, and would be equally worked upon, in this new state of things, in both cases. Accordingly we find, from Tertullian, in his "Soldier's Garland," that many in his time, immediately on their conversion, quitted the military service. We are told also, by Archelaus, who flourished under

Probus in the year 278, that many Roman soldiers, who had embraced Christianity, after having witnessed the piety and generosity of Marcellus, immediately forsook the profession of arms. We are told also by Eusebius, that, about the same time, "Numbers laid aside a military life, and became private persons, rather than abjure their religion." And here it may not be unworthy of remark, that soldiers, after their conversion, became so troublesome in the army, both on account of their scruples against the idolatrous practices required of the soldiery, and their scruples against fighting, that they were occasionally dismissed the service on these accounts.

SECT. III.

Objection to the foregoing statement, that the idolatry, which was then connected with the military service, and not the unlawfulness of war, was the reason why Christians declined it—Idolatry admitted to be a cause—Instance in Marinus—But the belief of the unlawfulness of fighting was another, and an equally powerful cause—Instances in Maximilian—Marcellus—Cassian—Marlin—The one scruple as much then a part of the Christian religion as the other.

As an objection may be made to the foregoing statement, I think it proper to notice it in this place.

It will be said, that the military oath, which all were obliged to take alike in the Roman armies, and which was to be repeated annually, was full of idolatry; that the Roman standards were all considered as gods, and had divine honours paid to them by the soldiery; and that the images also of the emperors, which were either fixed upon these standards, or placed in the midst of them in a temple in the camp, were to be adored in the same manner. Now these customs were interwoven with the military service. No Roman soldier was exempted from them. It will be urged, therefore, that no Christian could submit to these services. Indeed when a person was suspected of being a Christian in those times, he was instantly taken to the altars to sacrifice, it being notorious, that if he were a Christian he would not sacrifice, though at the hazard of his life. Is it not, therefore, to be presumed, that these idolatrous tests operated as the great cause, why Christians refused to enter into the army, or why they left it when converted as described in the former section?

That these tests operated as a cause, we must allow. And let this be considered as an insuperable argument against those, who contend that there were Christian soldiers in these times, for no Christian could submit to such idolatrous homage; but, if so, no Christian could be a soldier.

That these tests must have operated as a cause, we may infer from the history of Marinus. Marinus, according to Eusebius, was a man of family and fortune, and an officer in a legion, which, in the year 260, was stationed at Caesarea of Palestine. One of the centurion's rods happened to become vacant in this legion, and Marinus was appointed to it. But just at this moment another, next to him in rank, accused him before the tribunal of being a Christian, stating, that "the laws did not allow a Christian, who refused to sacrifice to the emperors, to hold any dignity in the army." Achæus, the judge, asked Marinus if it was true, that he had become a Christian. He acknowledged it. Three hours were then allowed him to consider, whether he would sacrifice or die. When the time was expired, he chose the latter. Indeed, so desirous were the early Christians of keeping clear of idolatry in every shape, that they avoided every custom that appeared in the least degree connected with it. Thus when a largess was given in honour of the emperors, L. Septimius Severus the father, and M. Aurelius Caracalla the son, a solitary soldier, as we learn from Tertullian, was seen carrying the garland, which had been given him on that occasion, in his hand, while the rest wore it upon their heads. On being interrogated by the commander, why he refused wearing it, he replied, that he had become a Christian. He was immediately punished before the army, and sent into prison. What became of him afterwards is not related. But it must be clear, if he lived and cherished his Christian feelings, that, when the day of the renewal of his oath, or of the worshipping of the standards, or of any sacrifice in the camp, should arrive, he would have refused these services, or abandoned his profession.

[Footnote 13: The priests wore the garland, when they sacrificed to the Heathen gods.]

But though unquestionably the idolatrous services, required of the soldiers of those times, hindered Christians from entering into the armies, and compelled those, who were converted in them, to leave them, nothing is more true, than that the belief, that it was unlawful for Christians to fight, occasioned an equal abhorrence of a military life. One of the first effects, which Christianity seems to have produced upon its first converts, when it was pure and unadulterated, and unmixed with the interpretations of political men, was a persuasion, that it became them, in obedience to the divine commands, to abstain from all manner of violence, and to become distinguishable as the followers of peace. We find accordingly from Athenagoras, and other early writers, that the Christians of his time, abstained, when they were struck, from striking again, and that they carried their principles so far, as even to refuse to go to law with those who injured them. We find also, from the same Athenagoras, and from Theophilus Antiochenus, Tatian, Minucius Felix, and others, that they kept away from the shews of the gladiators. This they did, not only because these shews were cruel; but because, as Theophilus says, "lest we should become partakers of the murders committed there." A similar reason is also given by Athenagoras on this occasion: "Who is there, says he, that does not prize the shews of the gladiators, which your emperors make for the people? But we, thinking that there is very little difference whether a man be the author or spectator of murder, keep away from all such sights." And here it may be observed, that the gladiators themselves were, generally prisoners of war, or reputed enemies, and that the murder of these was by public authority, and sanctioned; as in war, by the state. Now what conclusion are we to draw from these premises? Can we think it possible, that those, who refused to strike again, or to go to law with those who injured them, and who thought an attendance at the gladiatorial spectacles criminal on the principle, that he who stood by was a murderer, though the murder was sanctioned by law; should not have an objection to the military service, on the principle, that it was unlawful to fight?

In short, the belief of the unlawfulness of war, was universal among Christians in those times. Every Christian writer of the second century, who notices the subject, makes it unlawful for Christians to bear arms. And if the Christian writers of this age were of this opinion, contrary to all their sentiments before their conversion, and wholly from their knowledge of divine truths, why should not others, who had a common nature with these, be impressed, on receiving the same truths, in a similar manner? And so undoubtedly they were. And as this belief was universal among the Christians of those times, so it operated with them as an impediment to a military life, quite as much as the idolatry, that was connected with it, of which the following instances, in opposition to that of Marinus, may suffice.

The first case I propose to mention shall be, where there was an objection to entering into the military service upon this principle. And here, I apprehend none can be more in point than that of Maximilian, as preserved in the acts of Ruinart.

Maximilian, having been brought before the tribunal, in order to be enrolled as a soldier, Dion, the proconsul, asked him his name. Maximilian, turning to him, replied, "Why wouldst thou know my name? I am a Christian, and cannot fight."

Then Dion ordered him to be enrolled, and when he was enrolled, it was recited out of the register, that he was five feet ten inches high. Immediately after this, Dion bade the officer mark him. But Maximilian refused to be marked, still asserting that he was a Christian. Upon which Dion instantly replied, "Bear arms, or thou shalt die."

To this Maximilian answered, "I cannot fight, if I die. I am not a soldier of this world, but a soldier of God." Dion then said, "Who has persuaded thee to behave thus?" Maximilian answered, "My own mind, and he who called me." Dion then spoke to his father, and bade him persuade his son. But his father observed, that his son knew his own mind, and what it was best for him to do.

After this had passed, Dion addressed Maximilian again in these words, "Take thy arms, and receive the mark." "I can receive, says Maximilian, no such mark. I have already the mark of Christ." Upon which Dion said, "I will send thee quickly to thy Christ." "Thou mayest do so, said Maximilian, but the glory will be mine."

Dion then bade the officer mark him. But Maximilian still persisted in refusing, and spoke thus: "I cannot receive the mark of this world, and if thou shouldst give me the mark, I will destroy it. It will avail nothing. I am a Christian, and it is not lawful for me to wear such a mark about my neck, when I have received the saving mark of the Lord Jesus Christ, the Son of the living God, whom thou, knowest not, who died to give us life, and whom God gave for our sins. Him all we Christians obey. Him we follow as the restorer of our life, and the author of our salvation."

Dion instantly replied to this, "Take thy arms, and receive the mark, or thou shalt suffer a miserable death."—"But I shall not perish, said Maximilian. My name is already enrolled with Christ. I cannot fight."

Dion said, "Consider then thy youth, and bear arms. The profession of arms becomes a young man." Maximilian replied, "My arms are with the Lord. I cannot fight for any earthly consideration. I am now a Christian."

Dion the proconsul, said, "Among the life-guards of our masters Dioclesian and Maximian, and Constantius and Maximus, there are Christian soldiers, and they fight." Maximilian answered, "They know best what is expedient for them, but I am a Christian, and it is unlawful to do evil."

Dion said, "Take thy arms. Despise not the profession of a soldier, lest thou perish miserably."—"But I shall not perish, says Maximilian; and if I should leave this world, my soul will live with Christ the Lord."

Dion then ordered his name to be struck from the roll, and, when this was done, he proceeded, "Because, out of thy rebellious spirit, thou hast refused to bear arms, thou shall be punished according to thy deserts for an example to others." And then he delivered the following sentence: "Maximilian! because thou hast with a rebellious spirit refused to bear arms, thou art to die by the sword." Maximilian replied, "Thanks be to God."

He was twenty years, three months, and seventeen days old, and when he was led to the place of execution, he spoke thus: "My dear brethren, endeavour with all your might, that it may be your portion to see the Lord, and that he may give you such a crown;" and then, with a pleasant countenance, he said to his father, "Give the executioner the soldier's coat thou hast gotten for me, and when I shall receive thee in the company of the blessed martyrs, we may also rejoice together with the Lord."

After this he suffered. His mother Pompeiana obtained his body of the judge, and conveyed it to Carthage, and buried it near the place where the body of Cyprian the Martyr lay. And thirteen days after this his mother died, and was buried in the came place. And Victor, his father, returned to his habitation, rejoicing and praising God, that he had sent before such a gift to the Lord, himself expecting to follow after.

I shall only observe, upon this instance, that it is nearly pure and unmixed, or that it is but little connected with idolatrous circumstances, or rather, that the unlawfulness of fighting was principally urged by Maximilian as a reason against entering upon a military life. Let us now find a case, where, when a person was converted in the army, he left it, pleading this principle, as one among others, for his dereliction of it.

Marcellus was a centurion in the legion called "Trajana." On a festival, given in honour of the birth-day of Galerius, he threw down his military belt at the head of the legion, and in the face of the standards, declared with a loud voice, that he would no longer serve in the army, for that he had become a Christian. "I hold in detestation, said he, addressing himself to all the soldiers, the worship of your gods: gods, which are made of wood and stone, gods which are deaf and dumb." So far Marcellus, it appears, seems to have been influenced in his desertion of a military life by the idolatry connected with it. But let us hear him farther on this subject. "It is not lawful, says he, for a Christian, who is the servant of Christ the Lord, to bear arms for any earthly consideration." After a delay of more than three months in prison after this transaction, which delay was allowed for the purpose of sparing him, he was brought before the prefect. There he had an opportunity of correcting his former expressions. But as he persisted in the same sentiments, he suffered. It is remarkable, that, almost immediately after his execution, Cassian, who, was the notary to the same legion, refused to serve any longer, by publicly throwing his pen and accompt-book upon the ground, and declaring, at the same time, that the sentence of Marcellus was unjust. When taken up by the order of Aurelianus Agricolanus, he is described by the record, preserved by Ruinart, to have avowed the same sentiments as Marcellus, and, like him, to have suffered death.

It may not be necessary, perhaps, to cite any other instances, as opposed to that of Marinus, to the point in question. But, as another occurs, which may be related in few words, I will just mention it in this place. Martin, of whom

Sulpicius Severus says so much, had been bred to the profession of arms, but, on his conversion to Christianity, declined it. In the answer, which he gave to Julian the Apostate for his conduct on this occasion, we find him making use only of these words, "I am a Christian, and therefore I cannot fight."

Now this answer of Martin is detached from all notions of idolatry. The unlawfulness of fighting is given as the only motive for his resignation. And there is no doubt, that the unlawfulness of fighting was as much a principle of religion in the early times of Christianity, as the refusal of sacrifice to the Heathen gods; and that they operated equally to prevent men from entering into the army, and to drive them out of it on their conversion. Indeed these principles generally went together, where the profession of arms presented itself as an occupation for a Christian. He, who refused the profession on account of the idolatry connected with it, would have refused it on account of the unlawfulness of fighting. And he, who refused it on account of the guilt of fighting, would have refused it oh account of the idolatrous services it required. Both and each of them were impediments, in the early times of Christianity, to a military life.

SECT. IV.

Early Christians then declined the army on account, of one, among other persuasions, that it was unlawful for Christians to fight—Their practice examined farther, or into the fourth century—shewn from hence, that while Christianity continued pure, Christians still declined the military profession—but as it became less pure, their scruples against it became less—and when it became corrupt, their scruples against it ceased—Manner in which the Quakers make the practice of these early times support the meaning of the scriptural passages, which they adduce in favour of their tenet on war.

As it will now probably be admitted, that the early Christians refused to enter into the army, and that they left it after their conversion, on account of one, among other persuasions, that it was unlawful for them to fight, I must examine their practice, as it related to this subject, still farther, or I must trace it down to a later period, before I can show how the Quakers make the practice of these early times support the meaning of the scriptural passages, which they advance in favour of their tenet on war.

It may be considered as a well founded proposition, that, as the lamp of Christianity burnt bright, in those early times, so those, who were illuminated by it, declined the military profession; and, that, as its flame shone less clear, they had less objection to it. Thus, in the two first centuries, when Christianity was the purest, there were no Christian soldiers. In the third century, when it became less pure, there is frequent mention of such soldiers. And in the fourth, when its corruption was fixed,

Christians entered upon the profession of arms with as little hesitation, as they entered upon any other occupation in life.

That there were no Christian soldiers in the first and second centuries, has already been made apparent.

That Christianity also was purest in these times, there can be no doubt. Let us look at the character which is given of the first Christians by Athenagoras, Justin Martyr, Minucius Felix, and others of the early Christian writers. According to these they were plain and neat in their apparel, and frugal in their furniture. They were temperate in their eating and drinking. They relinquished all the diversions of the times, in which they saw any tendency to evil. They were chaste in their conversation, tempering mirth with gravity. They were modest and chaste in their deportment and manners. They were punctual to their words and engagements. They were such lovers of the truth, that, on being asked, if they were Christians, they never denied it, though death was the consequence of such a religious profession. They loved each other as brethren, and called one another by that name. They were kind, and courteous, and charitable, beyond all example, to others. They abstained from all manner of violence. They prayed for those who persecuted them. They were patterns of humility and patience. They made no sacrifice of their consciences, but would persevere in that which was right, never refusing to die for their religion. This is the character, which is uniformly given of them by the Christian writers of those times.

That their conduct was greatly altered in the third century, where we are now to view it, we may collect from indisputable authority. I stated in the former section, that a Christian soldier was punished for refusing to wear a garland, like the rest of his comrades, on a public occasion. This man, it appears, had been converted in the army, and objected to the ceremony on that account. Now Tertullian tells us, that this soldier was blamed for his unseasonable zeal, as it was called, by some of the Christians at that time, though all Christians before considered the wearing of such a garland as unlawful and profane. In this century there is no question but the Christian discipline began to relax. To the long peace the church enjoyed from the death of Antoninus to the tenth year of Severus, is to be ascribed the corruption that ensued. This corruption we find to have spread rapidly; for the same Tertullian was enabled to furnish us with the extraordinary instance of manufacturers of idols being admitted into the ecclesiastical order. Many corruptions are also noticed in this century by other writers. Cyprian complained of them, as they existed in the middle, and Eusebius, as they existed at the end of it, and both attributed it to the peace, or to the ease and plenty, which the Christians had enjoyed. The latter gives us a melancholy account of their change. They had begun to live in fine houses, and to indulge in luxuries. But, above all, they had begun to be envious, and quarrelsome, and to dissemble, and to cheat, and to falsify their word, so that they lost the character, which Pliny, an adversary to their religion, had been obliged to give of them, and which they had retained for more than a century, as appears by their own writers.

That there were Christian soldiers in this more corrupt century of the church, it is impossible to deny. For such frequent mention is made of them in the histories, which relate to this period, that we cannot refuse our assent to one or other of the propositions, either that there were men in the armies, who called themselves Christians, or that there were men in them, who had that name given them by others. That they were Christians, however, is another question. They were probably such Christians, as Dion mentioned to have been among the life-guards of Dioclesian and Maximian, and of Constantius and Maximus, of whom Maximilian observed, "These men may know what it is expedient for them to do, but I am a Christian, and therefore I cannot fight." Indeed, that real Christians could have been found in the army in this century is impossible, for the military oath, which was full of idolatry, and the adoration of the standards, and the performance of sacrifice, still continued as services not to be dispensed with by the soldiery. No one, therefore, can believe, that men in the full practice of Pagan idolatry, as every legionary soldier must then have been, were real Christians, merely because it is recorded in history, that men, calling themselves Christians, were found in the army in those times. On the other hand, if any soldiers professed Christianity at this period, or are related by authors to have professed it, and yet to have remained soldiers, it may be directly pronounced, that they could only have been nominal or corrupted Christians.

[Footnote 14: The military oath was not altered for Christians till the next century, when they were allowed to swear "by God, by Christ, and by the Holy Spirit, and by the majesty of the emperor, which, next to God, is to be loved and honoured by mankind."]

That Christianity was more degenerate in the fourth than in the third century (which is the next position) we have indubitable proof. One of the first facts, that strikes us, is an extraordinary one related by Lactantius, in his "Death of the persecuted," that there were Christians at this time, who, having probably a superstitious belief, that the sign of the Cross would be a preventive of pollution, were present, and even assisted at some of the Heathen sacrifices. But it is not necessary to detail these or other particulars. Almost every body knows, that more evils sprang up to the church in this century, than in any other, some of which remain at the present day. Indeed, the corruption of Christianity was fixed as it were by law in the age now mentioned. Constantine, on his conversion, introduced many of the Pagan ceremonies and, superstitions, in which he had been brought up, into the Christian religion. The Christians, rejoiced at seeing an emperor of their own persuasion, under whom they had hopes of restoration to equal privileges with others, and of freedom from persecution, submitted, in order to please or flatter him, to his idolatrous customs and opinions, thus sacrificing their consciences to their ease and safety. Many, on the other hand, who had always been Heathens, professed themselves Christians at once out of compliment to their emperor, and without any real conversion of the heart. Thus there was a mixture of Christianity and Paganism in the church, which had never been known before. Constantine too did not dispense with the blasphemous titles of Eternity, Divinity, and Pontifex Maximus, as they had been given to his predecessors. After his death, he was considered also as a god. And if Philostorgius is to be believed, the Christians, for so he calls them, prayed to and worshipped him as such.

Now in this century, when the corruption of the church may be considered to have been fixed, we scarcely find any mention of Christian soldiers, or we find the distinction between them and others gradually passing away. The truth is, that, when the Christians of this age had submitted to certain innovations upon their religion, they were in a fit state to go greater lengths; and so it happened, for as Heathens, who professed to be Christians out of compliment to their emperor, had no objection to the military service, so Christians, who had submitted to Heathenism on the same principle, relaxed, in their scruples concerning it. The latter too were influenced by the example of the former. Hence the unlawfulness of fighting began to be given up. We find, however, that here and there an ancient father still retained it as a religious tenet, but these dropping off one after another, it ceased at length to be a doctrine of the church.

Having now traced the practice of the Christians down to the fourth century, as far as the profession of arms is concerned, I shall state in few words the manner in which the Quakers make this practice support the meaning of the scriptural passages, which they produce in favour of their tenet on war.

The Quakers then lay it down as a position, that the Christians of the first and second centuries, as we had already observed, gave the same interpretation, as they themselves give, of the passages in question.

Now they say first, that if there were any words or expressions in the original manuscripts of the Evangelists or Apostles, which might throw light upon the meaning of these or other passages on the same subject, but which words and expressions were not in the copies which came after, then many of those who lived in the first and second centuries, had advantages with respect to knowledge on this subject, which their successors had not, inasmuch as the former were soon afterwards lost.

They say secondly, that if there was any thing in tradition which might help to explain these passages more satisfactorily, those of the first and second centuries had advantages again, because they lived nearer to these traditions, or to the time when they were more pure, than those Christians did, who succeeded them.

They say thirdly, that, if primitive practice be to be considered as the best interpreter of the passages in question, then those of the first and second centuries had their advantages again, because many of them lived in the times of the Evangelists and the Apostles, and all of them nearer to those who succeeded the Evangelists and Apostles, than those in the subsequent ages of the Christian era.

But in direct inference, they conceive, is to be drawn from these premises, namely, that the opinions of those who lived in the first and second centuries, relative to the meaning of the passages in question, are likely to be more correct on these several accounts, than those of Christians in any of the ages that followed.

And as in the first and second centuries of the church, when Christianity was purest, there were no Christian soldiers, but as in the fourth century, when it became corrupt, Christians had lost their objections to a military life, they conceive the opinions of the former to be more correct than those of the latter, because the opinions of real Christians, willing to make any sacrifice for their religion, must be always less biassed and more pure, than those of persons calling themselves Christians, but yet submitting to the idolatrous and other corrupt practices of the world.

And as they conceive this to be true of the opinions of the second century, when compared with those of the fourth, so they conceive it to be true of the opinions of the second, when compared with those of the moderns upon this subject, because, whatever our progress in Christianity may be, seeing that it is not equal to that of the first Christians, it is certain, besides the distance of time, that we have prejudices arising from the practice of fourteen centuries, during all which time it has been held out, except by a few individuals, as lawful for Christians to fight.

SECT. V.

Reflections of the author on the foregoing subject—Case of a superior being supposed, who should reside in the planet nearest to us, and see war carried on by men no larger than the race of ants—His enquiry as to the origin of these wars—their duration—and other circumstances—supposed answers to these questions—New arguments, from this supposed conversation, against war.

I have now stated the principal arguments, by which the Quakers are induced to believe it to be a doctrine of Christianity, that men should abstain from war, and I intended to close the subject in the last section. But when I consider the frequency of modern wars; when I consider that they are scarcely over, before others rise up in their place; when I consider again, that they come like the common diseases, which belong to our infirm nature, and that they are considered by men nearly in a similar light, I should feel myself criminal, if I were not to avail myself of the privilege of an author, to add a few observations of my own upon this subject.

Living as we do in an almost inaccessible island, and having therefore more than ordinary means of security to our property and our persons from hostile invasion, we do not seem to be sufficiently grateful to the Divine Being for the blessings we enjoy. We do not seem to make a right use of our benefits by contemplating the situation, and by feeling a tender anxiety for the happiness of others. We seem to make no proper estimates of the miseries of war. The latter we feel principally in abridgments of a pecuniary nature. But if we were to feel them in the conflagration of our towns and villages, or in personal wounds, or in the personal sufferings of fugitive misery and want, we should be apt to put a greater value than we do, upon the blessings of peace. And we should be apt to consider the connexion between war and misery, and between war and moral evil, in a light so much stronger than we do at present, that we might even suppose the precepts of Jesus Christ to be deficient, unless they were made to extend to wars, as well as to private injuries.

I wonder what a superior being, living in the nearest planet to our earth, and seeing us of the size of ants, would say, if he were enabled to get any insight into the nature of modern wars.

It must certainly strike him, if he were to see a number of such diminutive persons chasing one another in bodies over different parts of the hills and vallies of the earth, and following each other in little nut-shells, as it were upon the ocean, as a very extraordinary sight, and as mysterious, and hard to be explained. He might, at first, consider them as occupied in a game of play, or as emigrating for more food, or for a better climate. But when he saw them stop and fight, and destroy one another, and was assured that they were actually engaged in the solemn game of death, and this at such a distance from their own homes, he would wonder at the causes of these movements, and the reason of this destruction, and, not knowing that they possessed rational faculties, he would probably consider them as animals, destined by nature to live upon one another.

I think the first question he would ask would be, And from whence do these fightings come? It would be replied of course, that they came from their lusts; that these beings, though diminutive in their appearance, were men; that they had pride, and ambition; that they had envy and jealousy; that they indulged also hatred, and malice, and avarice, and anger; and that, on account of some or other of these causes, they quarrelled and fought with one another.

Well, but the superior being would say, is there no one on the earth, which I see below me, to advise them to conduct themselves better, or are the passions you speak of eternally uppermost, and never to be subdued? The reply would of course be, that in these little beings, called men, there had been implanted the faculty of reason, by the use of which they must know that their conduct was exceptionable, but that, in these cases, they seldom minded it. It would also be added in reply, that they had a religion, which was not only designed by a spirit from heaven, who had once lived among them, but had been pronounced by him as efficacious to the end proposed; that one of the great objects of this religion was a due subjugation of their passions; and this was so much insisted upon, that no one of them was considered to have received this religion truly, unless his passions were subdued. But here the superior being would enquire, whether they acknowledged the religion spoken of, and the authority from whence it came? To which it would of course be replied, that they were so tenacious of it, notwithstanding their indulgence of their passions, and their destruction of one another, that you could; not offend them more grievously than by telling them, that they did not belong to the religion they professed.

It is not difficult to foresee what other questions the superior being would ask, and probably the first of these would be, the duration of the lives of these little beings, and the length and frequency of their wars? It would be replied to this, that their lives were but as a vapour, which appeareth for a little time, and then vanisheth away, and that a quarter, and sometimes half of their time on earth, was spent in those destructive pursuits. The superior being would unquestionably be grieved at this account, because he would feel, that they really frustrated their own happiness, or that they lost by their own fault a considerable portion of the enjoyment of their lives.

In this impatience and anxiety for their future comfort, he would probably ask again, if they had any notion of any generous end for which they were born, for it is impossible they could suppose, that they came into the world to destroy one another. It would be replied, that they could not be ignorant of the true object or end; for the same religion, in which they believed, and which was said before to have been given them by a spirit sent from heaven, inculcated that they were sent there on a life of trial, and that in a future existence they were to give an account of their conduct, and were to be rewarded or punished accordingly. The same religion, it would be replied, also inculcated, notwithstanding their fightings, the utmost benevolence from one towards another. It wished so much every one of them to live peaceably, that it enjoined it as a duty rather to put up with an injury than to resent it, and it carried its benevolence so far, that it made no distinction between others of the same species, who spoke a different language, or lived in other districts or parts of the same world.

But here the superior being would interrupt.—What, he would say! Are they not to resent injuries, and yet do they go to war? And are they not afraid of fighting in this manner, when they are to give an account of their conduct in a future state? It would be replied, No: they have their philosophers among them, and most of these have determined, that, in this particular case, responsibility lies at the door of those who employ them. But, notwithstanding this, there are others living among them, who think otherwise. These are of opinion, that those who employ them cannot take the responsibility upon themselves without taking it from those whom they thus employ. But the religion of the Great Spirit no where says, that any constituted authorities among them can take away the responsibility of individual creatures, but, on the other hand, in the most positive terms, that every individual creature is responsible wholly for himself. And this religion does not give any creature an exemption on account of any force which may be used against him; because no one, according to its precepts, is to do evil, not even that good may come. But if he be persecuted, he is to adhere to that which is right, and to expect his reward in the other state. The impossibility, therefore, of breaking or dissolving individual responsibility, in the case of immoral action, is an argument to many, of the unlawfulness of these wars. And those who reason in this manner, think they have reasoned right, when they consider besides, that, if any of the beings in question were to kill one of his usually reputed enemies in the time of peace, he would suffer death for it, and be considered as accountable also for his crime in a future state. They cannot see, therefore, how any constituted authorities among them can alter the nature of things, or how these beings can kill others in time of war, without the imputation of a crime, whom they could not kill without such an imputation in time of peace. They see in the book of the Great Spirit no dispensation given to societies to after the nature of actions, which are pronounced to be crimes.

But the superior being would say, is it really defined, and is it defined clearly in the great book of the Spirit, that if one of them should kill another, he is guilty of a crime! It would be replied, not only of a crime, but of the greatest of all crimes, and that no dispensation is given to any of them to commit it in any case. And it would be observed farther, that there are other crimes, which these fightings generally include, which are equally specified and forbidden in the great book, but which they think it proper to sanction in the present case. Thus, all kinds of treachery and deceit are considered to be allowable, for a very ancient philosopher among them has left a maxim upon record, and it has not yet been beaten out of their heads, notwithstanding the precepts of the great book, in nearly the following words: "Who thinks of requiring open courage of an enemy, or that treachery is not equally allowable in war?"

[Footnote 15: Dolus an virtus quis in hoste requirat?]

Strange! the superior being would reply. They seem to me to be reversing the order of their nature, and the end of their existence. But how do they justify themselves on these occasions? It would be answered, that they not only justify themselves, but they even go so far as to call these fightings honourable. The greater the treachery, if it succeeds, and the greater the number of these beings killed, the more glorious is the action esteemed.

Still more strange! the superior being would reply. And is it possible, he would add, that they enter into this profession With a belief, that they are entering into an honourable employ? Some of them, it would be replied, consider it as a genteel employ. And hence they engage in it. Others, of a lazy disposition, prefer it to any other. Others are decoyed into it by treachery in various ways. There are also strong drinks, which they are fond of, and if they are prevailed upon to take these to excess, they lose their reason, and then they are obliged to submit to it. It must be owned too, that when these wars begin, the trades of many of these little beings are stopped, so that, to get a temporary livelihood, they go out and fight. Nor must it be concealed, that many are forced to go, both against their judgment and against their will.

The superior being, hurt at these various accounts, would probably ask, and what then does the community get by these wars, as a counterbalance for the loss of so much happiness, and the production of so much evil? It would be replied, nothing. The community is generally worse off at the end of these wars, than when it began to contend. But here the superior being would wish to hear no more of the system. He would suddenly turn away his face, and retire into one of the deep valleys of his planet, either with exclamations against the folly, or with emotions of pity for the situation, or with expressions of disgust at the wickedness, of these little creatures.

"O for a lodge in some vast wilderness,
Some boundless contiguity of shade,
Where rumour of oppression and deceit,
Of unsuccessful or successful war,
Might never reach me more! My ear is pain'd,
My soul is sick with every day's report,
Of wrong and outrage, with which earth is fill'd.

Lands, intersected by a narrow frith,
Abhor each other. Mountains interpos'd,
Make enemies of nations who had else,
Like kindred drops, been mingled into one.
Thus men devotes his brother, and destroys—
Then what is man? And what man, seeing this,
And having human feelings, does not blush,
And hang his head, to think himself a man?"

COWPER

SECT. VI.

Subject farther considered—Sad conceptions of those relative to the Divine Being, and the nature of the Gospel, who plead for the necessity of war—War necessary, where statesmen pursue the policy of the world—Nature and tendency of this policy—but not necessary where they pursue the policy of the Gospel—Nature and tendency of this policy—This tendency farther confirmed by a supposed case of a few Quakers becoming the governors of the world.

It is now an old maxim, and time with all its improvements has not worn it away, that wars are necessary in the present constitution of the world. It has not even been obliterated, that they are necessary, in order to sweep off mankind on account of the narrow boundaries of the earth. But they, who make use of this argument, must be aware, that, in espousing it, they declare no less, than that God, in the formation of his system, had only half calculated or half provided for its continuance, and that they charge him with a worse cruelty than is recorded of the worst of men: because, if he told men to increase and multiply, and gave them passions accordingly, it would appear as if he had created them only to enjoy an eternal feast in the sight of their destruction. Nor do they make him a moral governor of the world, if he allows men to butcher one another without an individual provocation or offence.

Neither do persons, arguing for the necessity of wars, do less than set themselves above the prophecies or oracles of God, which declare, that such warfare shall some time or other cease.

Neither do they, when they consider wars as necessary, and as never to be done away on account of the wicked passions of men, do less than speak blasphemy against the Gospel of Jesus Christ, because they proclaim it to be inadequate to the end proposed. For the proper subjugation of these, among other purposes, it was that the Gospel was promulgated. If it be thought a miracle, that the passions of men should be subdued, it is still a miracle, which Christianity professes to work; which it has worked since the hour of its institution; which it has worked in men, who have placed their highest reputation in martial glory; and which it continues to work, at the present day. Those, therefore, who promote wars, and excite the passions of men for this purpose, attempt to undo what it is the object of Christianity to do, and to stop the benign influence of the Gospel in the hearts of men.

That wars are necessary, or rather that they will be begun and continued, I do not mean to deny, while statesmen pursue the wisdom or policy of the world.

What this wisdom or policy is, it will not be difficult to trace. And first, when any matter is in dispute among the rulers of nations, is it not a maxim, that a high tone is desirable in the settlement of it, in order that the parties may seem to betray neither fear nor weakness, and that they may not be thought to lose any of their dignity or their spirit? Now as the human passions are constituted, except they have previously been brought under due regulation by Christianity, what is more likely than that a high tone of language on one side should beget a similar tone on the other, or that spirit, once manifested, should, produce spirit in return, and that each should fly off, as it were, at a greater distance from accommodation than before, and that, when once exasperation has begun, it should increase. Now what is the chance, if such policy be resorted to on such occasions, of the preservation of peace between them?

And, secondly, is it not also a received maxim, that, in controversies of this sort, a nation, even during the discussion, should arm itself, in order that it may shew itself prepared? But if any one nation arms during the discussion; if it fits out armies or fleets of observation with a view of deterring, or of being ready in case of necessity of striking, as it is called, the first blow; what is more probable, than that the other will arm also, and that it will fit out its own armies and fleets likewise? But when both are thus armed, pride and spirit will scarcely suffer them to relax, and what is then more probable, than that they will begin to fight?

And, thirdly, is it not a maxim also, that, even during the attempt to terminate the dispute, the public mind should be prepared? Are not the public papers let loose to excite and propagate a flame? And are not the deeds of our ancestors ushered into our ears to produce a martial spirit? But if the national temper is roused on both sides, and if preparations are carrying on at the same time with the utmost vigour, where again is the hope of the prevention of war between them?

And, fourthly, after hostilities are commenced, is it not a maxim also to perpetuate the enmity, which has been thus begun, and to give it a deeper root, and even to make it eternal by connecting it with religion? Thus flag-staffs are exhibited upon steeples, bells are rung to announce victories, and sermons are preached as occasions arise, as if the places allotted for Christian worship, were the most proper from whence to issue the news of human suffering, or to excite the passions of men for the destruction of one another. Nor is this all. The very colours of the armies are consecrated. I do not mean to say, that like the banners in the Praetorian tents, they are actually worshipped, but that an attempt is made to render them holy in the eyes of those who are present. An attempt is made, wonderful to relate, to incorporate war into the religion of Jesus Christ, and to perpetuate enmity on the foundation of the Gospel!

Now this is the policy of the world, and can it be seriously imagined, that such a system as this can ever lead to peace? For while discussions relative to matters of national dispute are carried on in a high tone, because a more humble tone would betray weakness or fear; while again, during this discussion, preparations for war are going on, because the appearance of being prepared would convey the idea of determined resolution, and of more than ordinary strength; while again, during the same discussion, the national spirit is awakened and inflamed; and while again, when hostilities have commenced, measures are resorted to, to perpetuate a national enmity, so that the parties consider themselves as natural enemies even in the succeeding peace, what hope is there of the extermination of war on earth?

But let us now look at the opposite policy, which is that of the Gospel. Now this policy would consist in the practice of meekness, moderation, love, patience, and forbearance, with a strict regard to justice, so that no advantages might be taken on either side. But if these principles, all of which are preventive of irritation, were to be displayed in our negotiations abroad, in the case of any matter in dispute, would they not annihilate the necessity of wars? For what is the natural tendency of such principles? What is their tendency, for instance, in private life? And who are the negotiators on these occasions but men? Which kind of conduct is most likely to disarm an opponent, that of him who holds up his arm to strike, if his opponent should not comply with his terms, or of him who argues justly, who manifests a temper of love and forbearance, and who professes that he will rather suffer than resist, and that he will do every thing sooner than that the affair shall not be amicably settled? The Apostle Paul, who knew well the human heart, says, "If thine enemy hunger, feed him, for in so doing thou shalt heap coals of fire on his head." That is, thou shall cause him, by thy amiable conduct, to experience burning feelings within himself, which, while they torment him with the wickedness of his own conduct, shall make him esteem thee, and bring him over to thy side. Thus thou shalt overcome his evil by thy good. Or, in other words, as fire melts the hardest metals, so thy kindness shall melt his anger. Thus Parnell—

"So artists melt the sullen ore of lead,
By heaping coals of fire upon its head.
Touch'd by the warmth, the metal teams to glow,
And pure from dress, the silver tang below."

This policy again would consist of the practical duty of attempting to tranquillize the minds of the people, while the discussion was going on, of exhorting them to await the event with composure, of declaring against the folly and wickedness of wars, as if peace only could be the result, of abstaining from all hostile preparations, and indeed from all appearance of violence. Now what influence would such conduct have again, but particularly when known to the opposite party? If the opposite party were to see those alluded to keeping down the passions of their people, would they inflame the passions of their own? If they were to be convinced, that these were making no preparations for war, would they put themselves to the expence of arming? Can we see any other termination of such a contest than the continuance of peace?

That the policy of the Gospel, if acted upon by statesmen, would render wars unnecessary, we may infer from supposed cases. And, first, I would ask this simple question, whether, if all the world were Quakers, there would be any more wars? I am sure the reply would be, no. But why not? Because nations of Quakers, it would be replied, would discuss matters in dispute between them with moderation, with temper, and with forbearance. They would never make any threats. They would never arm, and consequently they would never fight. It would be owing then to these principles, or, in other words, to the adoption of the policy of the Gospel in preference of the policy of the world, that, if the globe were to be peopled by Quakers, there would be no wars. Now I would ask, what are Quakers but men, and might not all, if they would suffer themselves to be cast in the same mould as the Quakers, come out of it of the same form and character?

But I will go still farther. I will suppose that any one of the four continents, having been previously divided into three parts, was governed only by three Quakers, and that these had the same authority over their subjects, as their respective sovereigns have at present. And I win maintain, that there would never be, upon this continent, during their respective administrations, another war. For, first, many of the causes of war would be cut off. Thus, for instance, there would be no disputes about insults offered to flags. There would be none again about the balance of power. In short, it would be laid down as a position, that no one was to do evil, that good might come. But as, notwithstanding, there might still be disputes from other causes, these would be amicably settled. For first, the same Christian disposition would be manifest in the discussion as in the former case. And, secondly, if the matter should be of an intricate nature, so that one Quaker government could not settle it with another, these would refer it, according to their constitution, to a third. This would be the "ne plus ultra" of the business. Both the discussion and the dispute would end here. What a folly then to talk of the necessity of wars, when, if but three Quakers were to rule a continent, they would cease there? There can be no plea for such language, but the impossibility of taming the human passions. But the subjugation of these is the immediate object of our religion. To confess, therefore, that wars must be, is either to utter a libel against Christianity, or to confess that we have not yet arrived at the stature of real Christians.

SECT. VII.

Subject farther examined—Case allowed, that if a cabinet of good men had to negotiate with a cabinet of good men, there might be no wars—but what would be the issue if good had to deal with bad—Case of American settlers, who adopted the policy of the world, and were always at war—and of other American settlers, who adopted the policy of the Gospel, and were always at peace—No case stronger, than where civilized men had to deal with savage American tribes.

I believe it will be allowed, that the Quaker instances, mentioned in the last section, are in point. But I am aware also, it will be said that, though different cabinets, all having the same Christian disposition, would settle their disputes in a friendly manner, how would a cabinet, consisting of spiritually minded men, settle with a cabinet of other men, who had not brought their passions under due regulation, and who, besides, had no notion of the unlawfulness of war.

I apprehend that it will not be denied, that men, as ferocious as any recorded in history, were those, who were found in America, when that continent was discovered. We hear nothing of Africans, or of Asiatics, which would induce us to suppose, that they were as wild and as barbarous as these. And nothing is more true of these, than they, were frequently concerned in wars. I shall therefore take these for an example, and I shall shew by the opposite conduct of two different communities towards them, that it rests with men to live peaceably or not, as they cultivate the disposition to do it, or as they follow the policy of the Gospel in preference of the policy of the world.

When the English, Dutch, and others, began to people America, they purchased land of the natives. But when they went to that continent, notwithstanding there were amiable persons among them, and friends to civil and religious liberty, they went with the notions of worldly policy, and they did not take with them the Christian wisdom of the unlawfulness of war. They acted on the system of preparation, because there might be danger. They never settled without palisadoes and a fort. They kept their nightly watches, though unmolested. They were, in short, in the midst of war, though no injury had been offered them by the natives, and though professedly in the midst of peace.

In the peopling of Connecticut, for I must begin with some one state, it was ordered at an English court, "holden at Dorchester, on the seventh day of June, 1736, that every town should keep a watch, and be well supplied with ammunition. The constables were directed to warn the watches in their turns, and to make it their care, that they should be kept according to the direction of the court. They were required also to take care that the inhabitants were well furnished with arms and ammunition, and kept in a constant state of defence." As these infant settlements, the author observes, "were filled and surrounded with numerous savages, the people conceived themselves in danger, when they lay down, and when they rose up, when they went out, and when they came in. Their circumstances were such, that it was judged necessary for every man to be a soldier."

[Footnote 16: Trumbull's History of Connecticut, p. 56.]

I find from this author, looking farther into his history, that previously to the order of the court at Dorchester, which did nothing more than enjoin a more strict execution of the original plan, which was that of military preparation and defence, some of the settlers had been killed by the natives. The provocation which the natives received, is not mentioned. But it was probably provocation enough to savage Indians, to see people settle in their country with all the signs and symptoms of war. Was such a system likely to have any other effect than that of exciting their jealousy? They could see that these settlers had at least no objection to the use of arms. They could see that these arms could never be intended but against other persons, and there were no other persons there but themselves. Judging therefore by outward circumstances, they could draw no inference of a peaceable disposition in their new neighbours. War soon followed. The Pequots were attacked. Prisoners were made on both sides. The Indians treated those settlers barbarously, who fell into their hands, for they did not see, on the capture of their own countrymen, any better usage on the part of the settlers themselves; for these settlers, again, had not the wisdom to use the policy of the Gospel, but preferred the policy of the world. "Though the first planters of New-England and Connecticut, says the same author, were men of eminent piety and strict morals, yet, like other good men, they were subject to misconception, and the influence of passion. Their beheading sachems whom they took in war, killing the male captives, and enslaving the women and children, was treating them with a severity, which, on the benevolent principles of Christianity, it will be difficult to justify."

[Footnote 17: P. 112.]

After this treatment, war followed war. And as other settlements were made by others in other states on the same principles, war fell to their portion likewise. And the whole history of the settlement of America, where these principles were followed, or where the policy of the world was adopted, is full of the wars between the settlers and the Indians, which have continued more or less, and this nearly up to the present day.

But widely different was the situation of the settlers under William Penn. When he and his fellow Quakers went to this continent, they went with the principles of Christian wisdom, or they adopted the policy of the Gospel instead of the policy of the world. They had to deal with the same savage Indians as the other settlers. They had the same fury to guard against, and were in a situation much more exposed to attack, and of course much more creative of alarm; for they had neither sword nor musket, nor pallisadoe, nor fort. They judged it neither necessary to watch, nor to be provided with ammunition, nor to become soldiers. They spoke the language of peace to the natives, and they proved the sincerity of their language by their continuance in a defenceless condition. They held out also, that all wars were unlawful, and that, whatever injuries were offered them, they would sooner bear them, than gratify the principle of revenge. It is quite needless to go farther into the system of this venerable founder of Pennsylvania. But it may be observed, that no Quaker settlers, when known to be such, were killed, and, whatever attacks were made upon the possessors of land in their neighbourhood, none were ever made upon those who settled on the lands purchased by William Penn.

[Footnote 18: "The Indians shot him who had the gun, says Storey in his Journal, and when they knew the young man they killed was a Quaker, they seemed sorry for it, but blamed him for carrying a gun. For they knew the Quakers would not fight, or do them any harm, and therefore, by carrying a gun, they took him for an enemy." This instance, which was in after times, confirms still more strongly all that has been said on this subject. Quakers at this time occasionally armed themselves against the wild beasts of the country.]

It may not be improper to observe farther, that the harmonious intercourse between the Quakers and the Indians continues uninterrupted to the present day. In matters of great and public concern, of which I could mention instances, it has been usual with the Indians to send deputies to the Quakers for advice, and the former have even been prevailed upon by the latter to relinquish wars, which they had it in contemplation to undertake. It is usual also for some of these to send their children to the Quakers for education. And so great is the influence of the Quakers over some of these tribes, that many individuals belonging to them, and now living together, have been reclaimed from a savage life. These have laid aside the toilsome occupations of the chase. They raise horses, cattle, and sheep. They cultivate wheat and flax. They weave and spin. They have houses, barns, and saw-mills among them. They have schools also, and civilization is taking place of the grossest barbarism.

These facts, when contrasted, speak for themselves. A cabinet of Quaker ministers, acting upon the policy of the Gospel, has been seated in the heart of a savage and warlike nation, and peace has been kept with them for ever. A cabinet of other settlers, acting on the policy of the world, has been seated in the heart of nations of a similar description, and they have almost constantly, been embroiled in wars. If Christian policy has had its influence on Barbarians, it would be libellous to say, that it would not have its influence upon those who profess to be Christians. Let us then again, from the instances which have been now recited, deprecate the necessity of wars. Let us not think so meanly of the Christian religion, as that it does not forbid, nor so meanly of its power, as that it is not ante to prevent, their continuance. Let us not think, to the disgrace of our religion, that the human heart, under its influence, should be so retrogade, that the expected blessing of universal peace should be thought no improvement in our moral condition, or that our feelings under its influence should continue so impure, that, when it arrives, we should regard it not so much a blessing, as a cures. But let us, on the other hand, hope and believe, that, as an opposite and purer policy is acted upon, it will do good to our own natures, good to the peace and happiness of the world, and honour to the religion of the Gospel.

SECT. VIII

Subject finally considered—Authors of wars generally justify their own as defensive—and state that, if any nation were to give up the practice of war, or to act on the policy of the Gospel, it would be overrun by others, which acted upon the policy of the world—Reason to believe, that such a nation would be held in veneration by others, and applied to by them for the settlement of their disputes—Sentiments of Bishop Butler in a supposed case—Case of Antoninus Pius—Conclusion.

Having now said all that I intended to say on the supposed necessity of wars, I shall for a short time direct the attention of the reader to two points, the only two, that I purpose to notice on this subject.

It is usually said, first, that the different powers, who go to war, give it out that their wars are defensive, or that they justify themselves on this principle.

I shall observe in reply to this, that it is frequently difficult to determine, where actual aggression begins. Even old aggressions, of long standing, have their bearings in these disputes. Not shall we find often any clue to a solution of the difficulty in the manifestoes of either party, for each makes his own case good in these; and if we were to decide on the merits of the question by the contents of these, we should often come to the conclusion, that both the parties were wrong. Thus, for instance, a notion may have been guilty of an offence to another. So far the cause of the other is a just one. But if the other should arm first, and this during an attempt at accommodation, it will be a question, whether it does not forfeit its pretensions to a just case, and whether both are not then to be considered as aggressors on the occasion?

When a nation avows its object in a war, and changes its object in the course of it, the presumption is, that such a nation has been the aggressor. And where any nation goes to war upon no other avowed principle, than that of the balance of power, such a nation, however right according to the policy of the world, is an aggressor according to the policy of the Gospel, because it proceeds upon the principle, that it is lawful to do evil, that good may come.

If a nation hires or employs the troops of another to fight for it, though it is not the aggressor in any war, yet it has the crime upon its head of making those aggressors, whom it employs.

But, generally speaking, few modern wars can be called defensive. A war, purely defensive, is that in which the inhabitants of a nation remain wholly at home to repel the attacks of another, and content themselves with sending protection to the settlements which belong to it. But few instance are recorded of such wars.

But if there be often a difficulty in discerning between aggressive and defensive wars, and if, moreover, there is reason to suppose, that most of the modern wars are aggressive, or that both patties become aggressors in the course of the dispute, it becomes the rulers of nations to pause, and to examine their own consciences with fear and trembling, before they allow the Sword to bedrawn, lest a dreadful responsibility should fall upon their heads for all the destruction of happiness, all the havoc of life, and all the slaughter of morals that may ensue.

It is said, secondly, that if any nation were publicly to determine to relinquish the practice if war, or to act on the policy of the Gospel, it would be overrun by other nations which might act on the policy of the world.

This argument is neither more nor less than that of the Pagan Celsus, who said in the second century, that, if the rest of the Roman empire were Christians, it would be overrun by the Barbarians.

Independently of the protection, which such a nation might count upon from the moral Governor of the world, let us enquire, upon rational principles, what would be likely to be its fate.

Armies, we know, are kept up by one nation, principally because they are kept up by another.

And in proportion as one rival nation adds to its standing armies, it is thought by the other to be consistent with the policy of the world to do the same. But if one nation were to decline keeping any armies at all, where would be the violence, to reason to suppose, that the other would follow the example? Who would not be glad to get rid of the expence of keeping them, if they could do it with safety? Nor is it likely, that any powerful nation, professing to relinquish war, would experience the calamities of it. Its care to avoid provocation would be so great, and its language would be so temperate, and reasonable, and just, and conciliatory, in the case of any dispute which might arise, that it could hardly fail of obtaining an accommodation. And the probability is, that such a nation would grow so high in esteem with other nations, that they would have recourse to it in their disputes with one another, and would abide by its decision. "Add the general influence, says the great Bishop Butler in his Analogy, which each a kingdom would have over the face of the earth, by way of example particularly, and the reverence which would be paid to it. It would plainly be superior to all others, and the world must gradually come under its empire, not by means of lawless violence, but partly by what must be allowed to be just conquest, and partly by other kingdoms submitting themselves voluntarily to it, throughout a course of ages, and claiming its protection one after another in successive exigencies. The head of it would be an universal monarch in another sense than any other mortal has yet been, and the eastern style would be literally applicable to him, "that all people, nations, and languages, should serve him." Now Bishop Butler supposes this would be the effect, where the individuals of a nation were perfectly virtuous. But I ask much less for my hypothesis. I only ask that the ruling members of the cabinet of any great nation (and perhaps these would only amount to three or four) should consist of real Christians, or of such men as would implicitly follow the policy of the Gospel, and I believe the result would be as I have described it.

Nor indeed are we without instances of the kind. The goodness of the emperor Antoninus Pius was so great, that he was said to have outdone all example. He had no war in the course of a long reign of twenty-four years, so that he was compared to Numa. And nothing is more true, than that princes referred their controversies to his decision.

Nor most I forget again to bring to the notice of the reader the instance, though on a smaller scale, of the colonists and descendants of William Penn. The Quakers have uniformly conducted themselves towards the Indians in such a manner, as to have given them from their earliest intercourse, an exulted idea of their character. And the consequence is, as I stated in a former section, that the former, in affairs of importance, are consulted by the latter at the present day. But why, if the cabinet of any one powerful nation were to act upon the noble principle of relinquishing war, should we think the other cabinets so lost to good feelings, as not to respect its virtue? Let us instantly abandon this thought; for the supposition of a contrary sentiment would make them worse than the savages I have mentioned.

Let us then cherish the fond hope, that human animosities are not to be eternal, and that man is not always to be made a tiger to man. Let us hope that the government of some one nation (and when we consider the vast power of the British empire, the nature of its constitution and religion, and the general humanity of its inhabitants, none would be better qualified than our own) will set the example of the total dereliction of wars. And let us, in all our respective situations, precede the anticipated blessing, by holding out the necessity of the subjugation of the passions, and by inculcating the doctrine of universal benevolence to man, so that when we look upon the beautiful islands, which lie scattered as so many ornaments of the ocean, we may wish their several inhabitants no greater injury than the violence of their own waves; or that, when we view continents at a distance from us, we may consider them as inhabited by our brothers; or that when we contemplate the ocean itself, which may separate them from our sight, we may consider it, not as separating our love, but as intended by Providence to be the means of a quicker intercourse for the exchange of reciprocal blessings.

CHAP. IV.

SECT. 1.

Fourth tenet is on the subject of a pecuniary maintenance of a Gospel ministry—Example and precepts of Jesus Christ—Also of Paul and Peter—Conclusions from these premises—These conclusions supported by the primitive practice—Great tenet resulting from these conclusions, and this primitive practice is, that the Quakers hold it unlawful to pay their own ministers, and also others of any other denomination, for their Gospel labours.

The fourth and last tenet of the Quakers is on the subject of the unlawfulness of a pecuniary maintenance of a Gospel ministry.

In explaining this tenet, I am aware that I am treading upon delicate ground. The great majority of Christians have determined, that the spiritual labourer is worthy of his hire; that if men relinquish the usual occupations by which a livelihood is obtained, in order that they may devote themselves to the service of religion, they are entitled to a pecuniary maintenance; and that, if they produce a rich harvest from what they sow, they are of all men, considering their usefulness to man to be greater in this than in any other service they can render him, the most worthy of encouragement and support. I am aware also of the possibility of giving offence to some in the course of the explanation of this tenet. To these I can only say, that I have no intention of hurting the feelings of any; that in the church there are those whom I esteem and love, and whom of all others I should be sorry to offend. But it must be obvious to these, and indeed to all, that it is impossible for me, in writing a history of the manners and opinions of the Quakers, to pass over in silence the tenet that is now before me; and if I notice it, they must be sensible, that it becomes me to state fully and fairly all the arguments which the Quakers give for the difference of opinion, which they manifest from the rest of their fellow-citizens, on this subject.

It does not appear then, the Quakers say, by any records that can be produced, that Jesus Christ ever received any payment for the doctrines which he taught, neither does it appear, as far as his own instructions, which are recorded by the Evangelists, can be collected on this subject, that he considered any pecuniary stipend as necessary or proper for those who were to assist in the promotion of his religion.

Jesus Christ, on the erection of his Gospel ministry, gave rules to his disciples, how they were to conduct themselves in the case before us. He enjoined the twelve, before he sent them on this errand, as we collect from

St. Matthew and St. Luke, that, "as they had received freely, so they were to give freely; that they were to provide neither gold, nor silver, nor brass in their purses, nor scrip, nor other things for their journey; for that the workman was worthy of his meat." And, on their return from their mission, he asked them, "When I sent you without purse, and scrip, and shoes, lacked ye any thing? And they said, nothing. Then said he unto them, but now he that hath a purse let him take it, and likewise his scrip."

[Footnote 19: Matt x. 8. Luke ix. 1.]

[Footnote 20: Luke xxii. 35.]

In a little time afterwards, Jesus Christ sent out other seventy as disciples, to whom he gave instructions similar to the former, that they should not take scrip, clothes, and money with them. But to these he said additionally, that "wheresoever they were received, they were to eat such things as were given them; but where they were not received, they were to go their way, and say, even the dust of your city, which cleaveth on us, we do wipe off against you." And as on that occasion he compared the ministers of his Gospel to the labourers, whom a man sends to the harvest, he told them they were at liberty to eat what was set before them, because the labourer was worthy of his hire.

[Footnote 21: Luke x.]

This the Quakers conceive to be the substance of all that Jesus Christ taught upon this subject. They go therefore next to St. Paul for a farther elucidation of it.

They are of opinion, that St. Paul, in his Epistle to Timothy, and to the Corinthians, and Galatians, acknowledges the position, that the spiritual labourer is worthy of his hire.

[Footnote 22: 1 Cor. ix.—1 Tim. v.—Gal. vi.]

The same Apostle, however, says, "that if any would not work, neither should he eat." From this text the Quakers draw two conclusions, first, that when ministers of the Gospel are idle, they are not entitled to bodily sustenance; and, secondly, that those only, who receive them, are expected to support them. The same Apostle says also, "Let him that is taught in the word, communicate unto him that teacheth in all good things," but he nowhere says, "to him that teacheth not."

[Footnote 23: 2 Thes. iii. 10.]

[Footnote 24: Gal. vi. 6.]

But though men, who faithfully spend their time in preaching the Gospel, are entitled to bodily maintenance from those who receive them, yet St.

Paul, the Quakers say, as far as his own practice was concerned thought it more consistent with the spirit of Christianity, and less detrimental to its interests, to support himself by the labour of his own hands, than to be supported by that of others. And he advises others to do the same, and not to make their preaching chargeable, "not because, says he we have not power, but to make ourselves an ensample to you to follow us."

[Footnote 25: 2 Thes. iii. 0.]

This power the Quakers consider ministers of the Gospel to abuse, who make their preaching chargeable, if by any means, they can support themselves; for St. Paul says farther, "What is my reward then? Verily that, when I preach the Gospel, I may make the Gospel of Christ without charge, that I abuse not my power in the Gospel." Thus the Apostle, they conceive, looks up to God and not to men for the reward of his spiritual labours. And the same Apostle makes it a characteristic of the false teachers, that they make merchandize of their hearers.

[Footnote 26: 1 Cor. ix. 18.]

[Footnote 27: 2 Pet. ii. 3.]

It is objected to the Quakers, on this occasion, that St. Paul received relief from the brethren at Philippi, as well as from others, when he did not preach. But their reply is, that this relief consisted of voluntary and affectionate presents sent to him in circumstances of distress. In this case the Apostle states, that he never desired these gifts, but that it was pleasant to him to see his religious instruction produce a benevolence of disposition that would abound to their account.

[Footnote 28: Philip. iv. 17.]

St. Peter is the only other person, who is mentioned in the New Testament as speaking on this subject. Writing to those, who had been called to the spiritual oversight of the churches, he advises as follows: "Feed the flock of God, which is among you, taking the oversight thereof not by constraint but willingly, not for filthy lucre, but of a ready mind, neither as being lords over God's heritage, but being examples to the flock. And when the chief Shepherd shall appear, ye shall receive a crown of glory that fadeth not away." Upon these words the Quakers make three observations; that ministers should not make a gain of the Gospel; that they should look to God for their reward, and not to men; and that Peter himself must have preached, like St. Paul, without fee or reward, or he could not consistently have recommended such a practice to others.

[Footnote 29: 1 Pet. v. 2.]

The Quakers, therefore, from the example and precepts of Jesus Christ, and of the Apostles Paul and Peter, come to the following conclusions on this subject. First, that God raises up his own ministers. Secondly, that these are to dispense his Gospel freely. Thirdly, that they are to take, whereever they are received, such things as are given them, which things they deserve while in the exercise of their calling, as much as the labourer his hire, but that no bargains are to be made about religion; that they are not to compel men to give, neither are they to take away any thing from those who are unwilling to receive them, but, in this case, to go their ways, and shake the dust from their feet against them, or, in other words, to declare that they have done their own duty in going to them with the word of God, and that the fault lies with them in refusing to hear it. Neither, when they return from their, missions, or are idle at home, are they to receive any thing, but to use their own scrips and purses, and clothes. And fourthly, that though it be lawful for them to receive such sustenance, under such limitations, during the exercise of their ministry, it would be more consistent with the spirit of Christianity, if they would give their spiritual labours freely, and look up to God for their reward, thus avoiding the character of false teachers, and the imputation of an abuse of their power in the Gospel.

Now these conclusions, the Quakers say, seem to have been sanctioned, in a great measure, by the primitive practice for the three first centuries of the church, or till the darkness of apostacy began to overwhelm the religious world.

In the very early times of the Gospel, many Christians, both at Jerusalem and Alexandria in Egypt, sold their possessions, and lived together on the produce of their common stock. Others in Antioch, Galatia, and Pontus, retained their estates in their possession, but established a fund, consisting of weekly or monthly offerings, for the support of the church. This fund continued in after times. But it was principally for the relief of poor and distressed saints, in which the ministers of the Gospel, if in that situation, might also share. Tertullian, in speaking of such funds, gives the following account: "Whatsoever we have, says he, in the treasury of our churches, is not raised by taxation, as though we put men to ransom their religion, but every man once a month, or when it pleaseth him, bestoweth what he thinks proper, but not except he be willing. For no man is compelled, but left free to his own discretion. And that, which is thus given, is not bestowed in vanity, but in relieving the poor, and upon children destitute of parents, and in the maintenance of aged and feeble persons, and of men wrecked by sea, and of such as have been condemned to metallic mines, or have been banished to islands, or have been cast into prison, professing the Christian faith."

In process of time, towards the close of the third century, some lands began to be given to the church. The revenue from these was thrown into the general treasury or fund, and was distributed, as other offerings were, by the deacons and elders, but neither bishops nor ministers of the Gospel were allowed to have any concern with it. It appears from Origen, Cyprian, Urban, Prosper, and others, that if in those times such ministers were able to support themselves, they were to have nothing from this fund. The fund was not for the benefit of any particular person. But if such ministers stood in need of sustenance, they might receive from it; but they were to be satisfied with simple diet, and necessary apparel. And so sacred was this fund held to the purposes of its institution, that the first Christian emperors, who did as the bishops advised them, had no recourse to it, but supplied the wants of ministers of the Gospel from their own revenues, as Eusebius, Theodoret, and Sozomen relate.

The council of Antioch, in the year 340, finding fault with the deacons relative to the management of the funds of the churches, ordained that the bishops might distribute them, but that they should take no part of them to themselves, or for the use of the priests and brethren who lived with them, unless necessity required it, using the words of the Apostle, "Having food and raiment, be therewith content."

In looking at other instances, cited by the Quakers, I shall mention one, which throws light for a few years farther upon this subject. In the year 359, Constantine, the emperor, having summoned a general council of bishops to Arminium in Italy, and provided for their subsistence there, the British and French bishops, judging it not fit to live on the public, chose rather to live at their own expence. Three only out of Britain, compelled by want, but yet refusing assistance offered to them by the rest, accepted the emperor's provision, judging it more proper to subsist by public than by private support. This delicate conduct of the bishops is brought to shew, that, where ministers of the Gospel had the power of maintaining themselves, they had no notion of looking to the public. In short, in those early times, ministers were maintained only where their necessities required it, and this out of the fund for the poor. Those, who took from the fund, had the particular application given them of "sportularii," or basket-clerks, because, according to Origen, Tertullian, Cyprian, and others, they had their portion of sustenance, given them in baskets. These portions consisted but of a small pittance, sufficient only for their livelihood, and were given them on the principle laid down by St. Matthew, that the ministers of Jesus Christ were to eat and drink only such things as were set before them.

In process of time new doctrines were advanced relative to the maintenance of the ministry, which will be hereafter explained. But as these were the inventions of men, and introduced during the apostacy, the Quakers see no reason, why they should look up to these in preference to those of Jesus Christ, and of the Apostles, and of the practice of Christians in the purest periods of the church. They believe, on the other hand, that the latter only are to be relied upon as the true doctrines. These were founded in divine wisdom on the erection of the Gospel ministry, and were unmixed with the inventions of men. They were founded on the genius and spirit of Christianity, and not on the genius or spirit of the world. The Quakers therefore, looking up to these as to the surer foundation, have adopted the following tenets on this subject.

They believe, first, that it would be inconsistent in them as Christians, to make a pecuniary payment to their own ministers for their Gospel labours. And they regulate their practice accordingly upon this principle. No one is ever paid by the Quakers for the performance of any office in the church. If a minister lives at home, and attends the meeting to which he belongs, he supports himself, as St. Paul did, by his own trade. If he goes on the ministry to other meetings, he is received by the Quakers as he travels along, and he finds meat and drink at the houses of these. His travelling expenses also are generally defrayed in this particular case. But he receives no reward, or fixed or permanent stipend, for his services on these or on any other such occasions.

And as the Quakers cannot pay their own ministers, so it is a tenet with them, that they cannot pay those of other denominations for their Gospel labours upon the same principle; that is, they believe, that all ministers of every description ought to follow the example, which St. Paul gave and enjoined them, of maintaining themselves by their own hands; they ought to look up to God and not to men for their reward; they ought to avoid the character of false teachers, and the imputation of abusing their power in the Gospel. And to these they add a particular reason, drawn from the texts quoted, which is not applicable in the former case, namely, that ministers are not authorised to take meat and drink from those who are not willing to receive them.

SECT. II.

Other reasons why Quakers cannot pay ministers of the Gospel of a different denomination from themselves—These arise out of the nature of the payments made to them, or out of the nature of tithes—History of tithes from the fourth century to the reign of Henry the eighth, when they were definitively consolidated into the laws of the land.

But the Quakers have other reasons, besides the general reasons, and the particular one which has been given, why as Christians they cannot pay ministers of a different denomination from themselves for their Gospel labours, or why they cannot pay ministers of the established church. These arise out of the nature of the payments which are made to them, or out of the nature of tithes. But to see these in their proper light, some notion should be given of the origin of this mode of their maintenance. I shall therefore give a very concise history of tithes from the fourth century, to which period I have already brought the reader, to the reign of Henry the eighth, when they took a station in the laws of the land, from which they have never yet been displaced.

It has already appeared that, between the middle and the close of the fourth century, such ministers of the Gospel as were able, supported themselves, but that those who were not able, were supported out of the fund for the poor. The latter, however, had no fixed or determined proportion of this fund allotted them, but had only a bare livelihood from it, consisting of victuals served out to them in baskets, as before explained. This fund too consisted of voluntary offerings, or of revenues from land voluntarily bequeathed. And the principle, on which these gifts or voluntary offerings were made, was the duty of charity to the poor. One material innovation, however, had been introduced, as I remarked before, since its institution, namely, that the bishops, and not the deacons, had now the management of this fund.

At the latter end of the fourth century, and from this period to the eighth, other changes took place in the system of which I have been speaking. Ministers of the Gospel began to be supported, all of them without distinction, from the funds of the poor. This circumstance occasioned a greater number of persons to be provided for than before. The people therefore were solicited for greater contributions than had been ordinarily given. Jerom and Omrysostom, out of good and pious motives, exhorted them in turn to give bountifully to the poor, and double honour to those who laboured in the lord's work. And though they left the people at liberty to bestow what they pleased, they gave it as their opinion, that they ought not to be less liberal than the ancient Jews, who, under the Levitical law, gave a tenth of their property to the priesthood and to the poor. Ambrose, in like manner, recommended tenths, as now necessary, and as only a suitable donation for these purposes.

The same line of conduct continued to be pursued by those who succeeded in the government of the church, by Augustin, bishop of Hippo, by Pope Leo, by Gregory, by Severin among the Christians, in Pannonia, and by others. Their exhortations, however, on this subject, were now mixed with promises and, threats. Pardon of sins and future rewards were held out on the one hand, and it was suggested on the other, that the people, themselves would be reduced to a tenth, and the blood of all the poor who died, would be upon their heads, if they gave less than a tenth of their incomes to holy uses. By exhortations of this sort, reiterated for three centuries, it began at length to be expected of the people, that they would not give less than tenths of what they possessed. No right however was alleged to such a proportion of their income, nor was coercion ever spoken of. These tenths also were for holy uses, which chiefly included the benefit of the poor. They were called the Lord's goods in consequence, and were also denominated the patrimony of the poor.

Another change took place within the period assigned, which I must now mention as of great concern. Ministers of the Gospel now living wholly out of the tenths, which with legacies constituted the fund of the poor, a determined portion of this fund, contrary to all former usage, was set apart for their use. Of this fund, one fourth was generally given to the poor, one fourth to the repairs of churches, one fourth to officiating ministers, and one fourth to the bishops with whom they lived. Hence the maintenance of ministers, as consisting of these two orders, and the repairs of churches, took now the greatest part of it, so that the face of things began to be materially altered. For whereas formerly this fund went chiefly to the poor, out of which ministers of the Gospel were provided, it now went chiefly to the church, out of which there came a provision for the poor. Another change also must be noticed with respect to the principle on which the gifts towards this fund were offered. For whereas tenths were formerly solicited on the Christian duty of charity to the poor, they were now solicited on the principle, that by the law of Moses they ought to be given for holy uses, in which the benefit of the fatherless, the stranger, and the widow, were included. From this time I shall use the word tithes for tenths, and the word clergy instead of ministers of the Gospel.

[Footnote 30: In process of time, as the bishops became otherwise provided for, the fund was divided into three parts for the other three purposes just mentioned.]

In the eighth century, matters were as I have now represented them. The people had been brought into a notion, that they were to give no less than a tenth of their income to holy uses. Bishops generally at this time, and indeed long previously to this, lived in monasteries. Their clergy lived also with them in these monasteries, and went from thence to preach in the country within the diocese. It must be also noticed, that there were, at this time, other monasteries under abbots or priors, consisting mostly of lay persons, and distinct from those mentioned, and supported by offerings and legacies in the same manner. The latter, however, not having numerous ecclesiastics to support, laid out more of their funds than the former were enabled to do, towards the entertainment of strangers, and towards the maintenance of the poor. Now it must be observed, that, when these two kinds of monasteries existed, the people were at liberty to pay their tithes to either of them as they pleased, and that, having this permission, they generally favoured the latter. To these they not only paid their tithes, but gave their donations by legacy. This preference of the lay abbies to the ecclesiastical arose from a knowledge that the poor, for whose benefit tithes had been originally preached up, would be more materially served. Other circumstances too occurred, which induced the people to continue the same preference. For the bishops in many places began to abuse their trust, as the deacons had done before, by attaching the bequeathed lands to their sees, so that the inferior clergy, and the poor became in a manner dependent upon them for their daily bread. In other places the clergy had seized all to their own use. The people therefore so thoroughly favoured the lay abbies in preference to those of the church, that the former became daily richer, while the, latter did little more than maintain their ground.

This preference, however, which made such a difference in the funds of the ecclesiastical, and of the lay monasteries, was viewed with a jealous eye by the clergy of those times, and measures were at length taken to remove it. In a council under Pope Alexander the third, in the year 1180, it was determined, that the liberty of the people should be restrained with respect to their tithes. They were accordingly forbidden to make appropriations to religious houses without the consent of the bishop, in whose diocese they lived. But even this prohibition did not succeed. The people still favoured the lay abbies, paying their tithes there, till Pope Innocent the third, in the year 1200, ordained, and he enforced it by ecclesiastical censures, that every one should pay his tithes to those who administered to him spiritual things in his own parish. In a general council also held at Lyons, in the year 1274, it was decreed, that it was no longer lawful for men to pay their tithes where they pleased, as before, but that they should pay them to mother church. And the principle, on which they had now been long demanded, was confirmed by the council of Trent under Pope Pius the fourth, in the year 1560, which was, that they were due by divine right. In the course of forty years after the payment of tithes had been forced by ecclesiastical censures and excommunications, prescription was set up. Thus the very principle, in which tithes had originated, was changed. Thus free will-offerings became dues, to be exacted by compulsion. And thus the fund of the poor was converted almost wholly into a fund for the maintenance of the church.

Having now traced the origin of tithes, as far as a part of the continent of Europe is concerned, I shall trace it as far as they have reference to our own country. And here I may instantly observe, and in a few words, that the same system and the same changes are conspicuous. Free will-offerings and donations of land constituted a fund for the poor, out of which the clergy were maintained. In process of time, tenths or tithes followed. Of these, certain proportions were allotted to the clergy, the repairs of the churches, and the poor. This was the state of things in the time of Offa, king of Mercia, towards the close of the eighth century, when that prince, having caused Ethelbert, king of the East Angles, to be treacherously murdered, fled to the Pope for pardon, to please whom, and to expiate his own sin, he caused those tithes to become dues in his own dominions, which were only at the will of the donors before.

About sixty years afterwards, Ethelwolf, a weak and superstitious prince, was worked upon by the clergy to extend tithes as dues to the whole kingdom; and he consented to it under the notion, that he was thus to avert the judgments of God, which they represented as visible in the frequent ravages of the Danes. Poor laymen, however, were still to be supported out of these tithes, and the people were still at liberty to pay them to whichever religious persons they pleased.

About the close of the tenth century, Edgar took from the people the right of disposing of their tithes at their own discretion, and directed that they should be paid to the parish churches. But the other monasteries or lay-houses resisting, his orders became useless for a time. At this period the lay monasteries were rich, but the parochial clergy poor. Pope Innocent, however, by sending out his famous decree before mentioned to king John, which was to be observed in England as well as in other places under his jurisdiction, and by which it was enacted, that every man was to pay his tithes to those only, who administered spiritual help to him in his own parish, settled the affair; for he set up ecclesiastical courts, thundered out his interdicts, and frightened both king and people.

[Footnote 31: To shew the principles, upon which princes acted with respect to tithes in these times, the following translation of a preamble to a grant of king Stephen may be produced: "Because, through the providence of Divine Mercy, we know it to be so ordered, and by the churches publishing it far and near, every body has heard, that, by the distribution of alms, persons may be absolved from the bonds of sin, and acquire the rewards of heavenly joys, I, Stephen, by the grace of God, king of England, being willing to have a share with those, who by a happy kind of commerce exchange heavenly things for earthly, and smitten with the love of God, and for the salvation of my own soul, and the souls of my father and mother, and all my forefathers and ancestors," &c.]

Richard the second confirmed these tithes to the parishes, as thus settled by this pope, but it was directed by an act, that, in all appropriations of churches, the bishop of the diocese should ordain a convenient sum of money to be distributed out of the fruits and profits of every living among the poor parishioners annually, in aid of their living and sustenance. "Thus it seems, says Judge Blackstone, the people were frequently sufferers by the withholding of those alms, for which, among other purposes, the payment of tithes was originally imposed." At length tithes were finally confirmed, and, in a more explicit manner, by the famous act of Henry the eighth on this subject. And here I must just observe, that, whereas from the eighth century to this reign, tithes were said to be due, whenever the reason of them was expressed, by divine right as under the Levitical law, so, in the preamble to the act of Henry the eighth, they are founded on the same principle, being described therein, "as due to God and the church." Thus, both on the continent of Europe, as well as in our own country, were these changes brought about, which have been described. And they were brought about also by the same means, for they were made partly by the exhortations and sermons of monks, partly by the decrees of popes, partly by the edicts of popish kings, and partly by the determinations of popish councils.

It is not necessary, that I should trace this subject farther, or that I should make distinctions relative to tithes, whether they may be rectorial, or vicarial, or whether they may belong to lay persons, I have already developed enough of their history for my purpose. I shall therefore hasten to state those other reasons, which the Quakers have to give, why they cannot pay other ministers of the Gospel for their spiritual labours, or rather, why they cannot consent to the payment of tithes, as the particular species of payment demanded by the church.

SECT. III

The other reasons then, as deducible from the history of tithes, are the following—First, that they are not in equity dues of the church—Secondly, that the payment of them being compulsory, it would, if acceded to, be an acknowledgment that the civil magistrate has a right to use force in matters of religion—And thirdly, that being claimed upon an act which holds them forth as of divine right, any payment of them would be an acknowledgment of the Jewish religion, and that Christ had not yet actually come.

The other reasons then, which the Quakers have to give for refusing to support other ministers of the Gospel, may be now deduced from the nature of tithes, as explained in the former section.

The early Quakers rejected the payment of tithes for three reasons; and, first, because they were demanded of them as dues of the church.

Against this doctrine, they set their faces as a religious body. They contended that, if they were due at all, they were due to the poor, from whom they had been forcibly taken, and to whom in equity they still belonged; that no prince could alter the nature of right and wrong that tithes were not justly due to the church, because Offa wished them to be so, to expiate his own crimes; or because Ethelwolf wished them to be so, from a superstitious notion, that he might thus prevent the incursions of the Danes; or because Stephen wished them to be so, as his own grant expresses, on the principle, that "the bonds of sin might be dissolved, and that he might have a part with those, who by a happy kind of commerce exchanged heavenly things for earthly;" or because the popes of Rome wished them to be so, from whose jurisdiction all the subjects of England were discharged by law.

They resisted the payment of them, because, secondly, tithes had become of a compulsory nature, or because they were compelled to pay them.

They contended on this head, that tithes had been originally free will-offerings, but that by violence they had been changed into dues, to be collected by force; that nothing could be more clear, than that ministers of the Gospel, if the instructions of Jesus to his disciples were to be regarded, were not authorized even to demand, much less to force, a maintenance from others; and that any constrained payment of these, while it was contrary to his intention, would be an infringement of their great tenet, by which they hold, that, Christ's kingdom being of a spiritual nature, the civil magistrate had no right to dictate a religion to any one, nor to enforce payment from individuals for the same, and that any interference in those matters, which were solely between God and man, was neither more nor less than an usurpation of the prerogative of God.

They resisted the payment of them, because, thirdly, they were demanded on the principle, as appeared by the preamble of the act of Henry the eighth, that they were due as under the Levitical law by divine right.

Against this they urged, first, that, if they were due as the Levitical tithes were, they must have been subject to the same conditions. They contended that, if the Levites had a right to tithes, they had previously given up to the community their own right to a share of the land, but that the clergy claimed a tenth of the produce of the lands of others, but had given up none of their own. They contended also, that tithes by the Levitical law were for the strangers, the fatherless, and the widows, as well as for the Levites, but that the clergy, by taking tithes, had taken that which had been for the maintenance of the poor, and had appropriated it solely to their own use, leaving them thus to become a second burthen upon the land.

But they contended, that the principle itself was false. They maintained, that the Levitical priesthood and tithes with it, had ceased on the coming of Jesus Christ, as appeared by his own example and that of his Apostles; that it became them, therefore, as Christians, to make a stand against this principle, for that, by acquiescing in the notion that the Jewish law extended to them, they conceived they would be acknowledging that the priesthood of Aaron still existed, and that Christ had not actually come.

This latter argument, by which it was insisted upon, that tithes ceased with the Jewish dispensation, and that those who acknowledged them, acknowledged the Jewish religion for Christians, was not confined to the early Quakers, but admitted among many other serious Christians of those times. The great John Milton himself, in a treatise which he wrote against tithes, did not disdain to use it. "Although, says he, hire to the labourer be of moral and perpetual right, yet that special kind of hire, the tenth, can be of no right or necessity but to that special labour for which God ordained it. That special labour was the Levitical and ceremonial service of the tabernacle, which is now abolished. The right, therefore, of that special hire, must needs be withal abolished, as being also ceremonial. That tithes were ceremonial is plain, not being given to the Levites till they had been first offered an heave offering to the Lord. He then, who by that law brings tithes into the Gospel, of necessity brings in withal a sacrifice and an altar, without which tithes by that law were unsanctified and polluted, and therefore never thought of in the first Christian times, nor till ceremonies, altars, and oblations had been brought back. And yet the Jews, ever since their temple was destroyed, though they have rabbies and teachers of their law, yet pay no tithes, as having no Levites to whom, no temple where, to pay them, nor altar whereon to hallow them; which argues, that the Jews themselves never thought tithes moral, but ceremonial only. That Christians therefore should take them up, when Jews have laid them down, must needs be very absurd and preposterous."

Having now stated the three great reasons, which the early Quakers gave, in addition to those mentioned in a former section, why they could not contribute towards the maintenance of an alien ministry, or why they could not submit to the payment of tithes, as the peculiar payment demanded by the established church, I shall only observe, that these are still insisted upon by their descendants, but more particularly the latter, because all the more, modern acts upon this subject take the act of Henry the eighth as the great ground-work or legal foundation of tithes, in the preamble of which it is inserted, that "they are due to God and the church." Now this preamble, the Quakers assert, has never been done away, nor has any other principle been acknowledged instead of that in this preamble, why tithes have been established by law. The Quakers therefore conceive, that tithes are still collected on the foundation of divine right, and therefore that it is impossible for them as Christians to pay them, for that by every such payment, they would not only be acknowledging the Jewish religion for themselves, but would be agreeing in sentiment with the modern Jews, that Jesus Christ has not yet made his appearance upon earth.

CHARACTER OF THE QUAKERS

CHAP. I.

Character of the Quakers—Character of great importance in life—yet often improperly estimated—This the case with that of the Quakers—Attempt to appreciate it duly— Many outward circumstances in the constitution of the Quakers, which may be referred to as certain helps in the promotion of this attempt.

Nothing is of more importance to an individual, than a good character, during life. Posthumous reputation, however desirable it may be thought, is of no service to the person whom it follows. But a living character, if it be excellent, is inestimable, on account of the good which it produces to him who possesses it. It procures him attention, civility, love, and respect from others. Hence virtue may be said to have its reward in the present life. This account will be also true of bodies, and particularly of religious bodies, of men. It will make a difference to the individuals of these, whether they be respected, as a body, by the individuals of other religious denominations, or by the government under which they live.

But though character be of so much importance in life, there are few who estimate it, either when they view it individually or collectively, as if really is. It is often, on the one hand, heightened by partiality, and, on the other, lowered by prejudice. Other causes also combine to afford wrong apprehensions concerning it. For as different diseases throw out often the same symptoms, and the judgment of the physician is baffled, so different motives produce frequently similar actions, and the man who tries to develop a character, even if he wishes to speak truth, finds himself at a loss to pronounce justly upon it.

As these failings and difficulties have attended men in estimating the character of individuals, so they seem to have attended those who have attempted to delineate that of the society of the Quakers. Indeed, if we were to take a view of the different traits which have been assigned to the latter, we could not but conclude, that there must have been some mistake concerning them. We should have occasion to observe, that some of these were so different in their kind, that they could not reasonably be supposed to exist in the same persons. We should find that others could scarcely be admitted among a body of professing Christians. The Quaker character, in short, as it has been exhibited to the world, is a strange medley of consistency and contradiction, and of merit and defect.

Amidst accounts, which have been so incongruous, I shall attempt the task of drawing the character of the Quakers. I shall state, first, all the excellencies, that have been said to belong to it. I shall state also, all the blemishes with which it has been described to be chargeable. I shall then enquire how far it is probable that any of these, and in what degree they are true. In this enquiry, some little reliance must be placed upon my personal knowledge of the Quakers, and upon my desire not to deceive. It is fortunate, however, that I shall be able, in this case, to apply to a test, which will be more satisfactory to the world, than any opinion of my own upon this subject. I mean to say that the Quakers, like others, are the creatures of their own education and habits, or that there are circumstances in their constitution, the knowledge of which will assist us in the discussion of this question; circumstances, which will speak for themselves and to which we way always refer in the case of difficulty or doubt. Their moral education, for example, which has been already explained, cannot but have an influence on the minds of those who receive it. Their discipline also, which has appeared to be of so extraordinary a nature, and to be conducted in so extraordinary a manner, cannot but have an effect of its own kind. The peculiar customs, in which they have been described to have been born and educated, and which must of course act upon them as a second nature, must have a correspondent influence again. From these, and other prominent and distinguishing features in their constitution, I may hope to confirm some of the truths which have been told, and to correct some of the errors that have been stated, on the subject which is now before us.

Nor am I without the hope, that the discussion of this subject upon such principles, will be acceptable to many. To those, who love truth, this attempt to investigate it will be interesting. To the Quakers it will be highly useful. For they will see, in the glass or mirror which I shall set before them, the appearance which they make in the world. And if they shall learn, in consequence, any of the causes either of their merits or of their failings, they will have learnt a lesson, which they may make useful by the farther improvement of their moral character.

CHAP. II.

Good part of the character of the Quakers—This general or particular—Great general trait is, that they are a moral people—This opinion of the world accounted for and confirmed by a statement of some of the causes that operate in the production of character—One of these causes is, the discipline peculiar to this society.

I come, according to my design, to the good part of the character of the Quakers. This may be divided into two sorts, into that which is general, and into that which is particular. On the subject of their general good character I shall first speak.

It is admitted by the world, as I had occasion to observe in the first chapter of the first volume, that whatever other objections might be brought against the Quakers as a body, they deserved the character of a moral people.

Though this fact be admitted, and there would therefore appear to be no necessity for confirming it, I shall endeavour, according to the plan proposed, to shew, by means of the peculiar system of the Quakers as a religious body, that this is one of the traits given them by the world, which cannot be otherwise than true.

The Quakers believe, in the first place, that the Spirit of God, acting in man, is one of the wises of virtuous character. They believe it to be, of all others, the purest and sublimest source. It is that spring, they conceive, to good action, and of course to exalted character, in which man can have none but a passive concern. It is neither hereditary nor factitious. It can neither be perpetuated in generation by the father to the child, nor be given by human art. It is considered by the Quakers as the great and distinguishing mark of their calling. Neither dress, nor language, nor peculiar customs, constitute the Quaker, but the spiritual knowledge which he possesses. Hence all pious men may be said to have been Quakers. Hence the patriarchs were Quakers, that is, because they professed to be led by the Spirit of God. Hence the Apostles and primitive Christians were Quakers. Hence the virtuous among the Heathens, who knew nothing of Christianity, were Quakers also. Hence Socrates may be ranked in profession with the members of this society. He believed in the agency of the Divine Spirit. It was said of him, "that he had the guide of his life within him; that this spirit furnished him with divine knowledge; and that it often impelled him to address and exhort the people." Justin the Martyr had no scruple in calling both Socrates and Heraclitus Christians, though they lived long before Christ; "for all such as these, says he, who lived according to the divine word within them, and which word was in all men, were Christians." Hence also, since the introduction of Christianity, many of our own countrymen have been Quakers, though undistinguished by the exterior marks of dress or language. Among these we may reckon the great and venerable Milton. His works are full of the sentiments of Quakerism. And hence, in other countries and in other ages, there have been men, who might be called Quakers, though the word Quakerism was unknown.

[Footnote 32: Milton not only considered the Spirit of God as a divine teacher, but that the scriptures were not to be spiritually understood but by the means of this spirit. He believed also, that human learning was not necessary for the qualification of a minister of the Gospel. And he wrote an essay against tithes.]

But independently of the agency of the Spirit of God, which the Quakers thus consider to be the purest cause of a good life and character, we may reckon a subordinate cause, which may be artificial, and within the contrivance and wisdom of man. When the early Quakers met together as a religious body, though they consisted of spiritually minded men, they resolved on a system of discipline, which should be followed by those who became members of the society. This discipline we have already seen. We have seen how it attempts to secure obedience to Christian precepts. How it marks its offences. How it takes cognizance of them when committed. How it tries to reclaim and save. How, in short, by endeavouring to keep up the members of the society to a good life, it becomes instrumental in the production or preservation of a good character.

From hence it will appear, that the virtue of the Quakers, and of course that their character may be distinguished into two kinds, as arising from two sources. It may arise from spiritual knowledge on the one hand, or from their discipline on the other. That which arises from the first, will be a perfect virtue. It will produce activity in excellence. That which arises from the second, will be inferior and sluggish. But, however it may be subject to this lower estimation, it will always be able to produce for those who have it, a certain degree of moral reputation in the opinion of the world.

These distinctions having been made as to the sources of virtuous character, there will be no difficulty in shewing, that the world has not been deceived in the point in question. For if it be admitted that the Divine Spirit, by means of its agency on the heart of man, is really a cause of virtuous character, it will then be but reasonable to suppose, that the Quakers, who lay themselves open for its reception more than others, both by frequent private retirements, and by their peculiar mode of public worship, should bear at least as fair a reputation as others, on account of the purity of their lives. But the discipline, which is unquestionably a guardian of morals, is peculiar to themselves. Virtue therefore is kept up among the Quakers by an extraordinary cause, or by a cause which does not act among many other bodies of men. It ought therefore to be expected, while this extraordinary cause exists, that an extraordinary result should follow, or that more will be kept apparently virtuous among the Quakers, in proportion to their numbers, than among those where no such discipline can be found, or, in other words, that, whenever the Quakers are compared with those of the world at large, they will obtain the reputation of a moral people.

CHAP. III.

SECT. I.

Particular traits in the Quaker character—The first of these is benevolence—This includes good will to man in his temporal capacity—Reasons why the world has bestowed this trait upon the Quakers—Probability of its existence—from their ignorance of many degrading diversions of the world—from their great tenet on war—from their discipline which inculcates equality—and watchfulness over morals—and from their doctrine that man is the temple of the Holy Spirit.

Of the good traits in the Quaker character, which may be called particular, I shall first notice that of benevolence. This benevolence will include, first, good will to man in his temporal capacity, or a tender feeling for him as a fellow creature in the varied situations of his life.

[Footnote 33: The reader must be aware, that all Quakers do not partake of this good part of the character. That the generality do, I believe. That all ought to do, I know, because their principles, as will be clearly seen, lead to such a character. Those, therefore, who do not, will see their own deficiency, or how much they have yet to attain, before they can become Quakers.]

The epithet of benevolent has been long given to this society. Indeed I know of no point, where the judgment of the world has been called forth, in which it has been more unanimous, than in the acknowledgment of this particular trait, as a part of the Quaker character.

The reasons for the application of this epithet to the society, may be various.

It has been long known, that as the early Christians called each other brethren, and loved each other as such, so there runs through the whole society of the Quakers a system of similar love, their affection for one another having been long proverbial.

It has been long known again, that as the early Christians extended their benevolence out of the pale of their own society to others who lived around them, so the Quakers manifest a similar disposition towards their countrymen at large. In matters of private distress, where persons of a different religious denomination have been the objects, and where such objects have been worthy, their purses have been generally open, and they have generally given as largely in proportion to their abilities as other people. To public charities in their respective places of residence, they have generally administered their proper share. But of late years, as they have mixed more with the world, this character of the society has become more conspicuous or better known. In the cases of dearth and distress, which happened a few years ago, it is a matter of publicity, that they were among the foremost in the metropolis, and in same other towns in the kingdom, not only in pecuniary contributions, but in frequent and regular attendances for the proper distribution of them. And if their character has ever stood higher for willingness to contribute to the wants of others at any one time than at another, it stands the highest, from whatever cause it may happen, at the present day.

It has been long known again, that as the early Christians extended their love beyond their own society, and beyond those of the world who lived around them, to those who were reputed natural enemies in their own times, so the Quakers do not confine their benevolence to their own countrymen, but extend it to the various inhabitants of the globe, without any discrimination, whether they are reputed hostile to the government under which they live. In times of war we never see them bearing arms, and in times of victory we never see them exulting, like other people. We never see them illuminating their houses, or running up and down the streets, frantic with joy upon such occasions. Their joy, on the other hand, is wounded by the melancholy consideration of the destruction of the human race, when they lament, with almost equal sympathy, over the slaughter of enemies and friends.

But this character of a benevolent people has been raised higher of late years in the estimation of the public by new circumstances or by the unanimous and decided part, which they have taken as a body, in behalf of the abolition of the slave-trade. For where has the injured African experienced more sympathy than from the hearts of Quakers? In this great cause the Quakers have been singularly conspicuous. They have been actuated as it were by one spring. In the different attempts, made for the annihilation of this trade, they have come forward with a religious zeal. They were at the original formation of the committee for this important object, where they gave an almost unexampled attendance for years. I mentioned in the preceding volume, that near a century ago, when this question had not awakened the general attention, it had awakened that of the Quakers as a body; and that they had made regulations in their commercial concerns with a view of keeping themselves clear of the blood of this cruel traffic. And from that time to the present day they have never forgotten this subject. Their yearly epistles notice it, whenever such notice is considered to be useful. And they hold themselves in readiness, on all fit occasions, to unite their efforts for the removal of this great and shocking source of suffering to their fellow-creatures.

But whether these be the reasons, or whether they be not the reasons, why the Quakers have been denominated benevolent, nothing is more true than that this appellation has been bestowed upon them, and this by the consent of their countrymen. For we have only to examine our public prints, to prove the truth of the assertion. We shall generally find there, that when there is occasion to mention the society, the word "benevolent" accompanies it.

The reader will perhaps be anxious to know how it happens, that the Quakers should possess this general feeling of benevolence in a degree so much stronger than the general body of their countrymen, that it should have become an acknowledged feature in their character. He will naturally ask, does their education produce it? Does their discipline produce it? Do their religious tenets produce it? What springs act upon the Quakers, which do not equally act upon other people? The explanation of this phenomenon will be perfectly consistent with my design; for I purpose, as I stated before, to try the truth or falsehood of the different traits assigned to the character of the Quakers, by the test of probabilities as arising from the nature of the customs or opinions which they adopt. I shall endeavour therefore to show, that there are circumstances, connected with their constitution, which have a tendency to make them look upon man in a less degraded and hostile, and in a more kindred and elevated light, than many others. And when I shall have accomplished this, I shall have given that explanation of the phenomenon, or that confirmation of the trait, which, whether it may or may not satisfy others, has always satisfied myself.

The Quakers, in the first place, have seldom seen a man degraded but by his vices. Unaccustomed to many of the diversions of the world, they have seldom, if ever, seen him in the low condition of a hired buffoon or mimic. Men, who consent to let others degrade themselves for their sport, become degraded in their turn. And this degradation increases with the frequency of the spectacle. Persons in such habits are apt to lose sight of the dignity of mankind, and to consider them as made for administration to their pleasures, or in an animal or a reptile light. But the Quakers, who know nothing of such spectacles, cannot, at least as far as these are concerned, lose either their own dignity of mind, or behold others lose it. They cannot therefore view men under the degrading light of animals for sport, or of purchasable play-things.

And as they are not accustomed to consider their fellow-creatures as below themselves, so neither are they accustomed to look with enmity towards them. Their tenet on the subject of war, which has been so amply detailed, prevents any disposition of this kind. For they interpret those words of Jesus Christ, as I have before shewn, which relate to injuries, as extending not to their fellow-citizens alone, but to every individual in the world, and his precept of loving enemies, as extending not only to those individuals of their own country, who may have any private resentment against them, but to those who become reputed enemies in the course of wars, so that they fix no boundaries of land or ocean, and no limits of kindred, to their love, but consider Jew and Gentile, Greek and Barbarian, bond and free, as their brethren. Hence neither fine nor imprisonment can induce them to learn the use of arms, so as to become qualified to fight against these, or to shed their blood. And this principle of love is not laid as it were upon the shelf, like a volume of obsolete laws, so that it may be forgotten, but is kept alive in their memories by the testimony which they are occasionally called to bear or by the sufferings they undergo by distraints upon their property, and sometimes by short imprisonments, for refusing military service.

But while these circumstances may have some influence in the production of this trait of benevolence to man in the character of the Quakers, the one by preventing the hateful sight of the loss of his dignity, and the other by destroying the seeds of enmity towards him, there are others, interwoven into their constitution, which will have a similar, though a stronger tendency towards it.

The great system of equality, which their discipline daily teaches and enforces, will make them look with an equal eye towards all of the human race. Who can be less than a man in the Quaker society, when the rich and poor have an equal voice in the exercise of its discipline, and when they fill equally the important offices that belong to it? And who is there out of the society, whom the Quakers esteem more than human? They bow their knees or, their bodies, as I have before noticed, to no man. They flatter no man on account of his riches or his station. They pay homage to no man on account of his rank or title. Stripped of all trappings, they view the creature man. If then they view him in this abstracted light, they can view him only as an equal. Bit in what other society is it, that a similar estimate is made of him? The world are apt in general to make too much of those in an elevated station, and those again in this station are apt to make less of others beneath them than they ought. Thus an under or an over valuation of individuals generally takes place in society; from whence it will unavoidably happen, that if some men are classed a little below gods, others will be classed but a little above the brutes of the field. Their discipline, again, has a tendency to produce in them an anxious concern for the good of their fellow-creatures. Man is considered, in the theory of this discipline, as a being, for whose spiritual welfare the members are bound to watch. They are to take an interest in his character and his happiness. If he be overtaken in a fault, he is not to be deserted, but reclaimed. No endeavour is to be spared for his restoration. He is considered, in short, as a creature, worthy of all the pains and efforts that can be bestowed upon him.

The religion of the Quakers furnishes also a cause, which occasions them to consider man in an elevated light. They view him, as may be collected from the preceding volume, as a temple of the Spirit of God. There is no man, so mean in station, who is not made capable by the Quakers of feeling the presence of the Divinity within him. Neither sect, nor country, nor colour, excludes him, in their opinion, from this presence. But it is impossible to view man as a tabernacle, in which the Divinity may reside, without viewing him in a dignified manner. And though this doctrine of the agency of the Spirit dwelling in man belongs to many other Christian societies, yet it is no where so systematically acted upon as by that of the Quakers.

These considerations may probably induce the reader to believe, that the trait of benevolence, which has been affixed to the Quaker character, has not been given it in vain. There can be no such feeling for the moral interests of man, or such a benevolent attention towards him in his temporal capacity, where men have been accustomed to see one another in low and degrading characters, as where no such spectacles have occurred. Nor can there be such a genuine or well founded love towards him, where men, on a signal given by their respective governments, transform their pruning-hooks into spears, and become tygers to one another without any private provocation, as where they can be brought under no condition whatever, to lift up their arm to the injury of any of the human race. There must, in a practical system of equality, be a due appreciation of man as man. There must, in a system where it is a duty to watch over him, for his good, be a tender attention towards him as a fellow creature. And in a system, which considers him as a temple in which the Divine Being may dwell, there must be a respect towards him, which will have something like the appearance of a benevolent disposition to the world.

SECT. II.

Trait of benevolence includes again good will towards man in his religious capacity— Quakers said to have no spirit of persecution, nor to talk with bitterness, with respect to other religious sects—This trait probable—because nothing in their doctrines that narrows love—their sufferings on the other hand—and their law against detraction— and their aversion to making religion a subject of common talk—all in favour of this trait.

The word benevolence, when mentioned as a trait in the character of the Quakers, includes also good will to man in his religious capacity.

It has often been observed of the Quakers, that they shew no spirit of persecution, and that you seldom hear them talk with bitterness, with respect to other religious societies.

On the first part of this trait it may be observed, that the Quakers have never had any great power of exercising dominion over others in matters of religion. In America, where they have had the greatest, they have conducted themselves well. William Penn secured to every colonist the full rights of men as to religious opinion and worship. If the spirit of persecution is ever to be traced to the Quakers, it must be found in their writings on the subject of religion. In one or two of the productions of their first authors, who were obliged to support their opinions by controversy, there is certainly an appearance of an improper warmth of temper; but it remarkable that, since these times, scarcely a book has appeal written by a Quaker against the religion of another. Satisfied with their own religious belief, they seem to have wished only to be allowed to enjoy it in peace. For when they have appeared as polemical writers, it has been principally in the defence of themselves.

On the second part of the trait I may remark, that it is possible, in the case of tithes, where their temper has been tried by expensive distraints, and hard imprisonments, that they may utter a harsh expression against a system which they believe to be anti-Christian, and which they consider also as repugnant to equity, inasmuch as it compels them to pay labourers, who perform work in their own harvest; but this feeling is only temporary, and is seldom extended beyond the object that produces it. They have never, to my knowledge, spoken with bitterness against churchmen on this account. Nor have I ever heard them, in such a season of suffering, pass the slightest reflection upon their faith.

That this trait of benevolence to man in his religious capacity is probably true, I shall endeavour to shew according to the method I have proposed.

There is nothing, in the first place, in the religious doctrines of the Quakers, which can produce a narrowness of mind in religion, or a contempt for the creeds of others. I have certainly, in the course of my life, known some bigots in religion, though, like the Quakers, I censure no man for his faith. I have known some, who have considered baptism and the sacrament of the supper as such essentials in Christianity, as to deny that those who scrupled to admit them, were Christians. I have known others pronouncing an anathema against persons, because they did not believe the atonement in their own way. I have known others again, who have descended into the greatest depths of election and reprobation, instead of feeling an awful thankfulness for their own condition as the elect, and the most tender and affectionate concern for those whom they considered to be the reprobate, indulging a kind of spiritual pride on their own account, which has ended in a contempt for others. Thus the doctrines of Christianity, wonderful to relate, have been made to narrow the love of Christians! The Quaker religion, on the other hand, knows no such feelings as these. It considers the Spirit of God as visiting all men in their day, and as capable of redeeming all, and this without any exception of persons, and that the difference of creeds, invented by the human understanding, will make no difference in the eternal happiness of man. Thus it does not narrow the sphere of salvation. It does not circumscribe it either by numerical or personal limits. There does not appear therefore to be in the doctrines of the Quaker religion any thing that should narrow their love to their fellow creatures, or any thing that should generate a spirit of rancour or contempt towards others on account of the religion they profess.

There are, on the contrary, circumstances, which have a tendency to produce an opposite effect.

I see, in the first place, no reason why the general spirit of benevolence to man in his temporal capacity, which runs through the whole society, should not be admitted as having some power in checking a bitter spirit towards him in his religious character.

I see again, that the sufferings, which the Quakers so often undergo on account of their religious opinions, ought to have an influence with them in making them tender towards others on the same subject. Virgil, who was a great master of the human mind, makes the queen of Carthage say to Aeneas, "Haud ignara mali, miseris succurrere disco," or, "not unacquainted with misfortunes myself, I learn to succour the unfortunate." So one would hope that the Quakers, of all other people, ought to know how wrong it is to be angry with another for his religion.

With respect to that part of the trait, which relates to speaking acrimoniously of other sects, there are particular circumstances in the customs and discipline of the Quakers, which seem likely to prevent it.

It is a law of the society, enforced by their discipline, as I shewed in a former volume, that no Quaker is to be guilty of detraction or slander. Any person, breaking this law, would come under admonition, if found out. This induces an habitual caution or circumspection in speech, where persons are made the subject of conversation. And I have no doubt that this law would act as a preventive in the case before us.

It is not a custom, again, with the Quakers, to make religion a subject of common talk. Those, who know them, know well how difficult it is to make them converse, either upon their own faith, or upon the faith of others. They believe, that topics on religion, familiarly introduced, tend to weaken its solemnity upon the mind. They exclude subjects also from ordinary conversation upon another principle. For they believe, that religion should not be introduced at these times, unless it can be made edifying. But, if it is to be made edifying, it is to come, they conceive, not through the medium of the activity of the imagination of man, but through the passiveness of the soul under the influence of the Divine Spirit.

SECT. III.

Trait of benevolence includes again a tender feeling toward the brute creation—Quakers remarkable for their tenderness to animals—This feature produced from their doctrine, that animals are not mere machines, but the creatures of God, the end of whose existence is always to be attended to in their treatment—and from their opinion as to what ought to be the influence of the Gospel, as recorded in their own summary.

The word benevolence, when applied to the character of the Quakers, includes also a tender feeling towards the brute creation.

It has frequently been observed by those who are acquainted with the Quakers, that all animals belonging to them are treated with a tender consideration, and are not permitted to be abused, and that they feel, in like manner, for those which may be oppressed by others, so that their conduct is often influenced in some way or other upon such occasions.

It will be obvious, in enquiring into the truth of this trait in the character of the Quakers, that the same principles, which I have described as co-operating to produce benevolence towards man, are not applicable to the species in question. But benevolence, when once rooted in the heart, will grow like a fruitful plant, from whatever causes it may spring, and enlarge itself in time. The man, who is remarkable for his kindness towards man, will always be found to extend it towards the creatures around him. It is an ancient saying, that "a righteous man regards the life of his beast, but the tender mercies of the wicked are cruel."

But, independently of this consideration, there is a principle in the Quaker constitution, which, if it be attended to, cannot but give birth to the trait in question.

It has been shewn in the first Volume, on the subject of the diversions of the field, that the Quakers consider animals, not as mere machines, to be used at discretion, but in the sublime light of the creatures of God, of whose existence the use and intention ought always to be considered, and to whom rights arise from various causes, any violation of which is a violation of a moral law.

This principle, if attended-to by the Quakers, must, as I have just observed, secure all animals which may belong to them, from oppression. They must so consider the end of their use, as to defend them from abuse. They must so calculate their powers and their years, as to shield them from excessive labour. They must so anticipate their feelings, as to protect them from pain. They must so estimate their instinct, and make an allowance for their want of understanding, as not to attach to their petty mischiefs the necessity of an unbecoming revenge. They must act towards them, in short, as created for special ends, and must consider themselves as their guardians, that these ends may not be perverted, but attained.

To this it may be added, that the printed summary of the religion of the society constantly stares them in the face, in which it is recorded, what ought to be the influence of Christianity on this subject. "We are also clearly of the judgment, that, if the benevolence of the Gospel were generally prevalent in the minds of men, it would even influence their conduct in the treatment of the brute creation, which would no longer groan, the victims of their avarice, or of their false ideas of pleasure."

CHAP. IV.

Second trait is that of complacency of mind or quietness of character—This trait confirmed by circumstances in their education, discipline, and public worship, which are productive of quiet personal habits—and by their disuse of the diversions of the world— by the mode of the settlement of their differences—by their efforts in the subjugation of the will—by their endeavour to avoid all activity of mind during their devotional exercises— all of which are productive of a quiet habitude of mind.

A second trait in the character of the Quakers is that of complacency, or evenness, or quietness of mind and manner.

This trait is, I believe, almost as generally admitted by the world, as that of benevolence. It is a matter of frequent observation, that you seldom see an irascible Quaker. And it is by no means uncommon to hear persons, when Quakers are the subject of conversation, talking of the mysteries of their education, or wondering how it happens, that they should be able to produce in their members such a calmness and quietness of character.

There will be no difficulty in substantiating this second trait.

There are circumstances, in the first place, in the constitution of the Quaker system, which, as it must have already appeared, must be generative of quiet personal habits. Among these may be reckoned their education. They are taught, in early youth, to rise in the morning in quietness, to go about their ordinary occupations in quietness, and to retire in quietness to their beds. We may reckon also their discipline. They are accustomed by means of this, when young, to attend the monthly and quarterly meetings, which are often of long continuance. Here they are obliged to sit patiently. Here they hear the grown up members of the society speak in order, and without any interruption of one another. We may reckon again their public worship. Here they are accustomed occasionally to silent meetings, or to sit quietly for a length of time, when not a word is spoken.

There are circumstances again in the constitution of the Quakers, which are either preventive of mental activity, and excitement of passion, or productive of a quiet habitude of mind. Forbidden the use of cards, and of music, and of dancing, and of the theatre, and of novels, it must be obvious, that they cannot experience the same excitement of the passions, as they who are permitted the use of these common amusements of the world. In consequence of an obligation to have recourse to arbitration, as the established mode of decision in the case of differences with one another, they learn to conduct themselves with temper and decorum in exasperating cases. They avoid, in consequence, the frenzy of him who has recourse to violence, and the turbid state of mind of him who engages in suits at law. It may be observed also, that if, in early youth, their evil passions are called forth by other causes, it is considered as a duty to quell them. The early subjugation of the will is insisted upon in all genuine Quaker families. The children of Quakers are rebuked, as I have had occasion to observe, for all expressions of anger, as tending to raise those feelings, which ought to be suppressed. A raising even of their voice is discouraged, as leading to the disturbance of their minds. This is done to make them calm and passive, that they may be in a state to receive the influence of the pure principle. It may be observed again, that in their meetings for worship, whether silent or vocal, they endeavour to avoid all activity of the mind for the same reason.

These different circumstances then, by producing quiet personal habits on the one hand, and quiet mental ones on the other, concur in producing a complacency of mind and manner, so that a Quaker is daily as it were at school, as far as relates to the formation of a quiet character.

CHAP. V.

Third trait is, that they do not temporize, or do that which they believe to be improper as a body of Christians—Subjects, in which this trait is conspicuous—Civil oaths—Holy or consecrated days—War—Tithes —Language—Address—Public illuminations—Utility of this trait to the Quaker character.

It is a third trait in the character of the Quakers, that they refuse to do whatever as a religious body they believe to be wrong.

I shall have no occasion to state any of the remarks of the world to shew their belief of the existence of this trait, nor to apply to circumstances within the Quaker constitution to confirm it. The trait is almost daily conspicuous in some subject or another. It is kept alive by their discipline. It is known to all who know Quakers. I shall satisfy myself therefore with a plain historical relation concerning it.

It has been an established rule with the Quakers, from the formation of their society, not to temporize, or to violate their consciences, or, in other words, not to do that which as a body of Christians they believe to be wrong, though the usages of the world, or the government of the country under which they live, should require it, but rather to submit to the frowns and indignation of the one, and the legal penalties annexed to their disobedience by the other. This suffering in preference of the violation of their consciences, is what the Quakers call "the bearing of their testimony," or a demonstration to the world, by the "testimony of their own example," that they consider it to be the duty of Christians rather to suffer, than to have any concern with that which they conceive to be evil.

The Quakers, in putting this principle into practice, stand, I believe, alone. For I know of no other Christians, who as a body pay this homage to their scruples, or who determine upon an ordeal of suffering in preference of a compromise with their ease and safety.

[Footnote 34: The Moravians, I believe, protest against war upon scriptural grounds. But how far in this, or in any other case, they bear a testimony, like the Quakers, by suffering, I do not know.]

The subjects, in which this trait is conspicuous, are of two kinds, first as they relate to things enjoined by the government, and secondly as they relate to things enjoined by the customs or fashions of the world.

In the first case there was formerly much more suffering than there is at present, though the Quakers still refuse a compliance with as many injunctions of the law as they did in their early times.

It has been already stated that they refused, from the very institution of their society, to take a civil oath. The sufferings, which they underwent in consequence, have been explained also. But happily, by the indulgence of the legislature, they are no longer persecuted for this scruple, though they still persevere in it, their affirmation having been made equal to an oath in civil cases.

It has been stated again, that they protested against the religious observance of many of those days, which the government of the country for various considerations had ordered to be kept as holy. In consequence of this they were grievously oppressed in the early times of their history. For when their shops were found open on Christmas day, and on Good Friday, and on the different fast-days which had been appointed, they were taken up and punished by the magistrates on the one hand, and insulted and beaten by the people on the other. But, notwithstanding this ill usage, they persevered as rigidly in the non-observance of particular days and times, as in their non-compliance with oaths, and they still persevere in it. It does not appear, however, that their bearing of their testimony in this case is any longer a source of much vexation or trouble to them: for though the government of the country still sanctions the consecration of particular days, and, the great majority of the people join in it, there seems, to have been a progressive knowledge or civilization in both, which has occasioned them to become tender on account of this singular deviation from their own practice.

But though the Quakers have been thus relieved by the legislature, and by the more mild and liberal disposition of the people, from so much suffering in bearing their testimony on the two occasions which have been mentioned, yet there are others, where the laws of government are concerned, on which they find themselves involved in a struggle between the violation of their consciences and a state of suffering, and where unfortunately there is no remedy at hand, without the manifestation of greater partiality towards them, than it may be supposed an equal administration of justice to all would warrant.

Hie first of these occasions is when military service, is enjoined. The Quakers, when drawn for the militia, refuse either to serve, or to furnish substitutes. For this refusal they come under the cognizance of the laws. Their property, where they have any, is of course distrained upon, and a great part of a little substance is sometimes taken from them on, this account. Where they have not distrainable property, which is occasionally the case, they never fly, but submit to the known punishment, and go patiently to prison. The legislature, however, has not been inattentive to the Quakers even upon this occasion; for it has limited their confinement to three months. The government also of the country afforded lately, in a case in which the Quakers were concerned, an example of attention to religious scruples upon this subject. In the late bill for arming the country *en masse*, both the Quakers and the Moravians were exempted from military service. This homage to religious principle did the authors of these exemptions the highest honour. And it certainly becomes the Quakers to be grateful for this unsolicited favour; and as it was bestowed upon them upon the full belief that they were the people they professed themselves, they should be particularly careful that they do not, by any inconsistency of conduct, tarnish the high reputation, which has been attached to them by the government under which they live.

The second occasion is, when tithes or other dues are demanded by the church. The Quakers refuse the payment of these upon principles, which have been already explained. They come of course again under the cognizance of the laws. Their property is annually distrained upon by warrant from justices of the peace, where the demand does not exceed the value of ten pounds, and this is their usual suffering in this case. But there have not been wanting instances where an unusual hardness, of heart has suggested a process, still allowable by the law, which has deprived them of all their property, and consigned them for life to the habitation of a prison.

[Footnote 35: One died, not a great while ago, in York Castle, and others, who were confined with him, would have shared his fate, but for the interference of the king.

It is surprising, that the clergy should not unite in promoting a bill in parliament, to extend the authority of the justices to grant warrants of distraint for tithes to more than the value of ten pounds, and to any amount, as this is the most cheap and expeditious way for themselves. If they apply to the ecclesiastical courts, they can enforce no payment of their tithes then. They can put the poor Quaker into prison, but they cannot obtain their debt. If they apply to the exchequer, they may find themselves, at the conclusion of their suit, and this after a delay of three years, liable to the payment of extra costs, to the amount of forty or fifty pounds, with which they cannot charge the Quaker, though they may confine him for life. Some, to my knowledge, have been glad to abandon these suits, and put up with the costs, incurred in them; rather than continue them. Recourse to such courts occasion the clergy frequently to be charged with cruelty, when, if they had only understood their own interests better, they would have avoided them.]

But it is not only in cases, of which the laws of the land take cognizance, that the Quakers prefer suffering to doing that which their consciences disapprove. There are other cases, connected, as I observed before, with the opinion of the world, where they exhibit a similar example. If they believe any custom or fashion of the world to be evil in itself, or to be attended with evil, neither popular applause nor popular fury can make them follow it, but they think it right to bear their testimony against it by its disuse, and to run the hazard of all the ridicule, censure, or persecution, which may await them for so doing.

In these cases, as in the former, it must be observed, that the sufferings of the Quakers have been much diminished, though they still refuse a compliance in as many instances as formerly, with the fashions of the world.

It was stated in the first volume, that they substituted the word Thou for You, in order that they might avoid by their words, as well as by their actions, any appearance of flattery to men. It was stated also, that they suffered on this account; that many magistrates, before whom they were carried in the early times of their institution, occasioned their punishment to be more severe, and that they were often abused and beaten by others, and put in danger of their lives. This persecution, however, for this singularity in their language, has long ceased; and the substitution of Thou for You is now only considered as an innocent distinction between Quakers and other people.

It was stated again in the same volume, that the Quakers abstained from the usual address of the world, such as from pulling off their hats, and from bowing the body, and from their ceremonious usages. It was explained also, that they did this upon two principles. First, because, as such ceremonies were no real marks of obeisance, friendship or respect, they ought to be discouraged by a people, whose religion required that no image should be held out, which was not a faithful picture of its original, and that no action should be resorted to, which was not correspondent with the feelings of the heart. Secondly, because all such ceremonies were of a complimentary or flattering nature, and were expressly forbidden by Jesus Christ. It was stated also, that, on account of their rejection of such outward usages, their hats were forcibly taken from their heads and thrown away; that they were beaten and imprisoned on this sole account; and that the world refused to deal with them as tradesmen, in consequence of which many could scarcely supply their families with bread. But this deviation from the general practice, though it still characterizes the members of this society, is no longer a source of suffering. Magistrates sometimes take care that their hats shall be taken gently from their heads on public occasions, and private persons expect now no such homage from Quakers, when they meet them.

There is, however, a custom, against which the Quakers anciently bore their testimony, and against which they continue to bear it, which subjects them occasionally to considerable inconvenience and loss. In the case of a general illumination, they never light up their houses, but have the courage to be singular in this respect, whatever may be the temper of the mob.

They believe that the practice of general illuminations cannot be adopted consistently by persons, who are lovers of the truth. They consider it as no certain criterion of joy. For, in the first place, how many light up their houses, whose hearts are overwhelmed with sorrow? And, in the second place, the event which is celebrated, may not always be a matter of joy to good minds. The birth-day of a prince, for example, may be ushered in as welcome, and the celebration of it may call his actions to mind, upon which a reflection may produce pleasure, but the celebration of the slaughter or devastation of mankind can afford no happiness to the Christian.

They consider the practice again, accompanied as it is with all its fiery instruments, as dangerous and cruel. For how many accidents have happened, and how many lives have been lost upon such occasions?

They consider it again as replete with evil. The wild uproar which it creates, the mad and riotous joy which it produces, the licentiousness which it favours, the invidious comparisons which it occasions, the partial favour which it fixes on individuals who have probably no moral merit, the false joys which it holds out, and the enmity which it has on some occasions a tendency to perpetuate; are so many additional arguments against it in the opinion of the Quakers.

For these and other reasons they choose not to submit to the custom, but to bear their testimony against it, and to run the hazard of having their windows broken, or their houses pillaged, as the populace may dictate: And in the same manner, if there be any other practice, in which the world may expect them to coincide, they reject it, fearless of the consequences, if they believe it to be productive of evil.

This noble practice of bearing testimony, by which a few individuals attempt to stem the torrent of immorality by opposing themselves to its stream, and which may be considered as a living martyrdom, does, in a moral point of view, a great deal of good to those, who conscientiously adopt it. It recalls first principles to their minds. It keeps in their remembrance the religious rights of man. It teaches them to reason upon principle, and to make their estimates by a moral standard. It is productive both of patience and of courage. It occasions them to be kind and attentive, and merciful to those who are persecuted and oppressed. It throws them into the presence of the Divinity when they are persecuted themselves. In short, it warms their moral feelings, and elevates their religious thoughts.

Like oil, it keeps them from rusting. Like a whetstone, it gives them a new edge. Take away this practice from the constitution of the Quakers, and you pull down a considerable support of their moral character. It is a great pity that, as professing Christians, we should not, more of us, incorporate this noble principle individually into our religion. We concur unquestionably in customs, through the fear of being reputed singular, of which our hearts do not always approve, though nothing is more true, than that a Christian is expected to be singular with respect to the corruptions of the world. What an immensity of good would be done, if cases of persons, choosing rather to suffer than to temporize, were so numerous as to attract the general notice of men! Would not every case of suffering operate as one of the most forcible lessons that could be given to those who should see it? And how long would that infamous system have to live, which makes a distinction between political expediency and moral right?

CHAP. VI.

A fourth trait is, that, in political affairs, they reason upon principle, and not from consequences—This mode of reasoning insures the adoption of the maxim of not doing evil that good may come—Had Quakers been legislators, many public evils had been avoided, which are now known in the world—Existence of this trait probable from the influence of the former trait—and from the influence of the peculiar customs of the Quakers—and from the influence of their system of discipline upon their minds.

The next trait, which I shall lay open to the world as belonging to the Quaker character, is, that in all those cases, which may be called political, the Quakers generally reason upon principle, and but seldom upon consequences.

I do not know of any trait, which ever impressed me more than this in all my intercourse with the members of this society. It was one of those which obtruded itself to my notice on my first acquaintance with them, and it has continued equally conspicuous to the present time.

If an impartial philosopher, from some unknown land, and to whom our manners, and opinions, and history, were unknown, were introduced suddenly into our metropolis, and were to converse with the Quakers there on a given political subject, and to be directly afterwards conveyed to the west end of the town, and there to converse with politicians, or men of fashion, or men of the world, upon the same, he could not fail to be greatly surprised. If he thought the former wise, or virtuous, or great, he would unavoidably consider the latter as foolish, or vicious, or little. Two such opposite conclusions, as he would hear deduced from the reasonings of each, would impress him with an idea, that he had been taken to a country inhabited by two different races of men. He would never conceive, that they had been educated in the same country, or under the same government. If left to himself, he would probably imagine, that they had embraced two different religions. But if he were told that they professed the same, he would then say, that the precepts of this religion had been expressed in such doubtful language, that they led to two sets of principles contradictory to one another. I need scarcely inform the reader, that I allude to the two opposite conclusions, which will almost always be drawn, where men reason from motives of policy or from moral right.

If it be true that the Quakers reason upon principle in political affairs, and not upon consequences, it will follow as a direct inference, that they will adopt the Christian maxim, that men ought not to do evil that good may come. And this is indeed the maxim, which you find them adopting in the course of their conversation on such subjects, and which I believe they would have uniformly adopted, if they had been placed in political situations in life. Had the Quakers been the legislators of the world, we should never have seen many of the public evils that have appeared in it. It was thought formerly, for example, a glorious thing to attempt to drive Paganism from the Holy Land, but Quakers would never have joined in any of the crusades for its expulsion. It has been long esteemed, again, a desideratum in politics, that among nations, differing in strength and resources, a kind of balance of power should be kept up, but Quakers would never have engaged in any one war to preserve it. It has been thought again, that it would contribute to the happiness of the natives of India, if the blessings of the British constitution could be given them instead of their own. But Quakers would never have taken possession of their territories for, the accomplishment of such a good. It has been long thought again a matter of great political importance, that our West-Indian settlements should be cultivated by African labourers. But Quakers would never have allowed a slave-trade for such a purpose. It has been thought again, and it is still thought, a desirable thing, that our property should be secured from the petty depredations of individuals. But Quakers would never have consented to capital punishments for such an end. In short, few public evils would have arisen among mankind, if statesmen had adopted the system, upon which the Quakers reason in political affairs, or if they had concurred with an ancient Grecian philosopher in condemning to detestation the memory of the man, who first made a distinction between expediency and moral right.

That this trait of reasoning upon principle, regardless of the consequences, is likely to be a feature in the character of the Quakers, we are warranted in pronouncing, when we discover no less than three circumstances in the constitution of the Quakers, which may be causes in producing it.

[Footnote 36: The Sierra Leone Company, which was founded for laudable purposes, ought have been filled by Quakers; but when they understood that there was to be a fort and depot of arms in the settlement, they declined becoming proprietors.]

This trait seems, in the first place, to be the direct and legitimate offspring of the trait explained in the last chapter. For every time a Quaker is called upon to bear his testimony by suffering, whether in the case of a refusal to comply with the laws, or with the customs and fashions of the land, he is called upon to refer to his own conscience, against his own temporal interest, and against the opinion of the world. The moment he gives up principle for policy in the course of his reasoning upon such occasions, then he does as many others do, that is, he submits to the less inconvenience, and then he ceases to be a Quaker. But while he continues to bear his testimony, it is a proof that he makes expediency give way to what he imagines to be right. The bearing therefore of testimony, where it is conscientiously done, is the parent, as it is also the bulwark and guardian of reasoning upon principle. It throws out a memento whenever it is practised, and habituates the subject of it to reason in this manner. But this trait is nourished and supported again by other causes, and first by the influence, which the peculiar customs of the Quakers must occasionally have upon their minds. A Quaker cannot go out of doors, but he is reminded of his own singularity, or of his difference in a variety of respects from his fellow-citizens. Now every custom, in which he is singular, whether it be that of dress or of language, or of address, or any other, is founded, in his own mind, on moral principle, and in direct opposition to popular opinion and applause. He is therefore perpetually reminded, in almost all his daily habits, of the two opposite systems of reasoning, and is perpetually called upon as it were to refer to the principles, which originally made the difference between him and another citizen of the world.

Neither has the discipline of the Quakers a less tendency to the production of the trait in question. For the business, which is transacted in the monthly and quarterly and yearly meetings, is transacted under the deliberations of grave and serious men, who consider themselves as frequently under the divine influence, or as spiritually guided on such occasions. In such assemblies it would be thought strange if any sentiment were uttered, which savoured of expediency in opposition to moral right. The youth therefore, who are present, see no other determination of any question than by a religious standard. Hence these meetings operate as schools, in which they are habituated to reason upon principle, and to the exclusion of all worldly considerations, which may suggest themselves in the discussion of any point.

CHAP. VII.

A fifth trait is, that they have an extraordinary independence of mind—This probable, because the result of the farmer trait—because likely to be produced by their discipline— by their peculiar custom—and by their opinions on the supposed dignity of situations in life—because again, they are not vulnerable by the seduction of governments—or by the dominion of the church—or by the power of fashion and of the opinion of the world.

The next trait, conspicuous in the character of the Quakers, and which is nearly allied to the former, is that of independence of mind.

This trait is of long standing, having been coeval with the society itself. It was observed by Cromwell, that "he could neither win the Quakers by money, nor by honours, nor by places, as he could other people." A similar opinion is entertained of them at the present day. For of all people it is generally supposed that they are the least easily worked upon, or the least liable to be made tools or instruments in the bands of others. Who, for example, could say, on any electioneering occasion, whatever his riches might be, that he could command their votes?

There will be no difficulty in believing this to be a real feature in the character of the Quakers. For when men are accustomed to refer matters to their reason, and to reason upon principle, they will always have an independence of mind, from a belief that they are right. And wherever it be a maxim with them not to do evil that good may come, they will have a similar independence from a consciousness, that they have never put themselves into the power of the world. Hence this independence of mind must be a result of the trait explained in the former chapter.

But in looking into the constitution of the Quakers, we shall find it full of materials for the production of this noble trait.

Their discipline has an immediate tendency to produce it. For in no community does a man feel himself so independent as a man. A Quaker is called upon in his own society to the discharge of important offices. He sits as a representative, a legislator, and a judge. In looking round him, he finds all equal in privileges, but none superior, to himself.

Their peculiar customs have the same tendency, for they teach them to value others, who are not of the society, by no higher standard than that by which they estimate themselves. They neither pull off their hats, nor bow, nor scrape. In their speech they abstain from the use of flattering words and of titles. In their letters, they never subscribe themselves the humble servants of any one. They never use, in short, any action or signature, which, serving as a mark of elevation to others, has any influence towards the degradation of themselves.

Their opinions also upon the supposed dignity of situations in life contribute towards the promotion of this independence of their minds.

They value no man, in the first place, on account of his earthly title. They pay respect to magistrates, and to all the nobility of the land, in their capacity of legislators, whom the chief magistrate has appointed; but they believe that the mere letters in a schedule of parchment can give no more intrinsic worth to a person, than they possess themselves, and they think with Juvenal, that "the only true nobility is virtue." Hence titles, in the glare of which some people lose the dignity of their vision, have no magical effect upon Quakers.

They value no man again on account of the antiquity of his family exploits. They believe, that there are people now living in low and obscure situations, whose ancestors performed in the childhood of history, when it was ignorant and incapable of perpetuating traditions, as great feats as those, which in its greater maturity it has recorded. And as far as these exploits of antiquity may be such as were performed in wars, they would not be valued by them as ornaments to men, of whose worth they can only judge by their virtuous or their Christian character.

They value no man again on account of the antiquity of his ancestry. Believing revelation to contain the best account of the rise of man, they consider all families as equally old in their origin, because they believe them to have sprung from the same two parents, as their common source.

But this independence of mind, which is said to belong to the Quakers, may be fostered again by other circumstances, some of which are peculiar to themselves.

Many men allow the independence of their minds to be broken by an acceptance of the honours offered to them by the governments, under which they live; but no Quaker could accept of any of the honours of the world.

Others allow the independence of their minds to be invaded by the acceptance of places and pensions from the same quarter. But Quakers, generally speaking, are in a situation too independent in consequence of their industry, to need any support of this kind; and no Quaker could accept it on the terms on which it is usually given.

Others again suffer their opinions to be fettered by the authority of ecclesiastical dominion, but the Quakers have broken all such chains. They depend upon no minister of the Gospel for their religion, nor do they consider the priesthood, as others do, as a distinct order of men.

Others again come under the dominion of fashion and of popular opinion, so that they dare only do that which they see others do, or are hurried from one folly to another, without having the courage to try to resist the stream. But the life of a Quaker is a continual state of independence in this respect, being a continual protest against many of the customs and opinions of the world.

I shall now only observe upon this subject, that this trait of independence of mind, which is likely to be generated by some, and which is preserved by other of the causes which have been mentioned, is not confined to a few members, but runs through the society. It belongs to the poor as well as to the rich, and to the servants of a family as well as to those who live in poverty by themselves. If a poor Quaker were to be introduced to a man of rank, he would neither degrade himself by flattery on the one hand, nor by any unbecoming submission on the other. He would neither be seduced into that which was wrong, nor intimidated from doing that which was right, by the splendour or authority of appearances about him. He would still preserve the independence of his mind, though he would behave with respect. You would never be able to convince him, that he had been talking with a person, who had been fashioned differently from himself. This trait of independence cannot but extend itself to the poor. For having the same rights and privileges in the discipline, and the same peculiar customs, and the same views of men and manners as the rest of the society, a similar disposition must be found in these, unless it be counteracted by other causes. But as Quaker servants, who live in genuine Quaker families, wear no liveries, nor any badges of poverty or servitude, there is nothing in the opposite scale to produce an opposite feature in their character.

CHAP. VIII.

SECT. I.

A sixth trait is that of courage—This includes, first, courage in life—Courage not confined to military exploits—Quakers seldom intimidated or abashed—dare to say what they think—and to do what they believe to be right—This trait may arise from that of bearing their testimony—and from those circumstances which produced independence of mind—and from the peculiar customs of the society.

Another trait in the character of the Quakers, which is nearly allied to independence of mind, is courage. This courage is conspicuous both in life and in the hour of death. That, which belongs to the former instance, I shall consider first.

If courage in life were confined solely to military exploits, the Quakers would have no pretensions to this character. But courage consists of presence of mind in many situations of peril different from those in war. It consists often in refusing to do that which is wrong, in spite of popular opinion. Hence the man, who refuses a challenge, and whom men of honour would brand with cowardice on that account, may have more real courage in so doing, and would have it in the estimation of moral men, than the person who sends it. It may consist also in an inflexible perseverance in doing that which is right, when persecution is to follow. Such was the courage of martyrdom. As courage then may consist in qualities different from that of heroism, we shall see what kind of courage it is that has been assigned to the Quakers, and how far they may be expected to be entitled to such a trait.

There is no question, in the first place, that Quakers have great presence of mind on difficult and trying occasions. To frighten or to put them off their guard would be no easy task. Few people have ever seen an innocent Quaker disconcerted or abashed.

They have the courage also to dare to say, at all times and in all places, what they believe to be right.

I might appeal for the truth of this, as far as the early Quakers are concerned, to the different conversations which George Fox had with Oliver Cromwell, or to the different letters which be wrote to him as protector, or to those which he afterwards wrote to king Charles the second.

I might appeal again to the address of Edward Burroughs to the same monarch.

I might appeal again to the bold but respectful language, which the early Quakers used to the magistrates, when they were carried before them, and to the intrepid and dignified manner in which they spoke to their judges, in the coarse of the numerous trials to which they were brought in those early times.

I might appeal also to Barclay's address to the king, which stands at the head of his Apology.

"As it is inconsistent, says Barclay to king Charles the second, with the truth I bear, so it is far from me to use this letter as an engine to flatter thee, the usual design of such works, and therefore I can neither dedicate it to thee, nor crave thy patronage, as if thereby I might have more confidence to present it to the world, or be more hopeful of its success. To God alone I owe what I have, and that more immediately in matters spiritual, and therefore to him alone, and the service of his truth, I dedicate whatever work he may bring forth in me, to whom only the praise and honour appertain, whose truth needs not the patronage of worldly princes; his arm and power being that alone by which it is propagated, established, and confirmed."

And farther on, he says, "Thou hast tasted of prosperity and adversity; thou knowest what it is to be banished thy native country, to be overruled, as well as to rule, and to sit upon the throne; and, being oppressed, thou hast reason to know how hateful the oppression is both to God and man. If, after all these warnings and advertisements, thou dost not turn unto the Lord with all thy heart, but forget him who remembered thee in distress, and give up thyself to follow lust and vanity; surely great will be thy condemnation."

And this courage to dare to say what they believe to be right, as it was an eminent feature in the character of the primitive, so it is unquestionably a trait in that of the modern Quakers. They use no flattery even in the presence of the king; and when the nation has addressed him in favour of new wars, the Quakers have sometimes had the courage to oppose the national voice on such an occasion, and to go before the same great personage, and in a respectful and dignified manner, to deliver a religious petition against the shedding of human blood.

They have the courage also to dare to do as well as to say what they consider to be right.

It is recorded of the early Quakers, that, in the times of the hottest persecution, they stood to their testimony in the places appointed for their worship. They never assembled in private rooms, or held private conventicles, employing persons to watch at the doors, to keep out spies and informers, or to prevent surprise from the magistrates. But they worshipped always in public, and with their doors open. Nor, when armed men were sent to dissolve their meetings, did they ever fly, but, on the summons to break up and depart, they sat motionless, and, regardless of threats and blows, never left their devotions, but were obliged to be dragged out, one by one, from their places. And even when their meeting-houses were totally destroyed by the magistrates, they sometimes met the next meeting-day, and worshipped publicly on the ruins, notwithstanding, they knew that they were subject by so doing, to fines, and scourges, and confinements, and banishment, and that, like many others of their members who had been persecuted, they might die in prison.

This courage of the early Quakers has descended as far as circumstances will allow us to judge, to their posterity, or to those who profess the same faith. For happily, on account of the superior knowledge which has been diffused among us since those times, and on account of the progress of the benign influence of Christianity, both of which may be supposed to have produced among the members of our legislature a spirit of liberality in religion, neither the same trials; nor the same number of them, can be afforded for the courage of the modern Quakers, as were afforded for that of the Quakers of former days. But as far as there are trials, the former exhibit courage proportioned to their weight. This has been already conspicuous in the bearing of their testimony, either in those cases where they run the hazard of suffering by opposing the customs of the world, or where, by refusing a compliance with legal demands which they believe to be antichristian, they actually suffer. Nor are these sufferings often slight, when we consider that they may be made, even in these days of toleration, to consist of confinement, as the law now stands, for years, and it may happen even for life, in prison.

This trait of courage in life, which has been attached to the character of the Quakers, is the genuine offspring of the trait of "the bearing of their testimony." For by their testimony it becomes their religion to suffer, rather than comply with many of the laws and customs of the land. But every time they get through their sufferings, if they suffer conscientiously, they gain a victory, which gives them courage to look other sufferings in the face, and to bid defiance to other persecutions.

This trait is generated again by all those circumstances which have been enumerated, as producing the quality of independence of mind, and it is promoted again by the peculiar customs of the society. For a Quaker is a singular object among his countrymen. His dress, his language, and his customs mark him. One person looks at him. Another perhaps derides him.

He must summon resolution, or he cannot stir out of doors and be comfortable. Resolution, once summoned, begets resolution again, till at length he acquires habits superior to the looks and frowns, and ridicule, of the world.

SECT. II.

The trait of courage includes also courage in death—This trait probably—from the lives which the Quakers lead—and from circumstances connected with their religious faith.

The trait of courage includes also courage in death, or it belongs to the character of the Quakers, that they shew great indifference with respect to death, or that they possess great intrepidity, when sensible of the approach of it.

I shall do no more on this subject, than state what may be the causes of this trait.

The dissolution of all our vital organs, and of the cessation to be, so that we move no longer upon the face of the earth, and that our places know us no more, or the idea of being swept away suddenly into eternal oblivion, and of being as though we had never been, cannot fail of itself of producing awful sensations upon our minds. But still more awful will these be, where men believe in a future state, and where, believing in future rewards and punishments, they contemplate what may be their allotment in eternity. There are considerations, however, which have been found to support men, even under these awful reflections, and to enable them to meet with intrepidity their approaching end.

It may certainly be admitted, that, in proportion as we cling to the things of the world, we shall be less willing to leave them, which may induce an appearance of fear with respect to departing out of life; and that, in proportion as we deny the world and its pleasures, or mortify the affections of the flesh, we shall be more willing to exchange our earthly for spiritual enjoyments, which may induce an appearance of courage with respect to death.

It may be admitted again, that, in proportion as we have filled our moral stations in life, that is, as we have done justly, and loved mercy, and this not only with respect to our fellow-creature man, but to the different creatures of God, there will be a conscious rectitude within us, which will supply us with courage, when we believe ourselves called upon to leave them.

It may be admitted again, that, in proportion as we have endeavoured to follow the divine commands, as contained in the sacred writings, and as we have followed these through faith, fearless of the opinions and persecutions of men, so as to have become sufferers for the truth, we shall have less fear or more courage, when we suppose the hour of our dissolution to be approaching.

Now, without making any inviduous comparisons, I think it will follow from hence, when we consider the Quakers to be persons of acknowledged moral character, when we know that they deny themselves for the sake of becoming purer beings, the ordinary pleasures and gratifications of the world, and when almost daily experience testifies to us, that they prefer bearing their testimony, or suffering as a Christian body, to a compliance with customs, which they conceive the Christian religion to disapprove, that they will have as fair pretensions to courage in the hour of death, as any other people, as a body, from the same causes.

There are other circumstances, however, which may be taken into consideration in this account, and, in looking over these, I find none of more importance than those which relate to the religious creeds which may be professed by individuals or communities of men.

Much, in the first place, will depend upon the circumstance, how far men are doubtful and wavering in their creeds, or how far they depend upon others for their faith, or how far, in consequence of reasoning or feeling, they depend upon themselves. If their creeds are not in their own power, they will be liable to be troubled with every wind of doctrine that blows, and to be unhappy, when the thought of their dissolution is brought before them. But the Quakers, having broken the power or dominion of the priesthood, what terrors can fanaticism hold out to them, which shall appal their courage in their later hours?

It is also of great importance to men what may be the nature of their creeds. Some creeds are unquestionably more comfortable to the mind than others. To those, who believe in the doctrine of election and reprobation, and imagine themselves to be of the elect, no creed can give greater courage in the hour of death; and to those who either doubt or despair of their election, none can inspire more fear. But the Quakers, on the other hand, encourage the doctrine of perfection, or that all may do the will of God, if they attend to the monitions of his grace. They believe that God is good, and just, and merciful; that he visits all with a view to this perfection without exception of persons; that he enables all, through the sacrifice of Christ, to be saved; and that he will make an allowance for all according to his attributes; for that he is not willing that any should perish, but that all should inherit eternal life.

CHAP. IX.

Last good trait is that of punctuality to words and engagements—This probable from the operation of all those principles, which have produced for the Quakers the character of a moral people—and from the operation of their discipline.

The last good trait, which I shall notice in the character of the Quakers, is that of punctuality to their words and engagements.

This is a very ancient trait. Judge Forster entertained this opinion of George Fox, that if he would consent to give his word for his appearance, he would keep it. Trusted to go at large without any bail, and solely on his bare word, that he would be forth coming on a given day, he never violated his promise. And he was known also to carry his own commitment himself. In those days also, it was not unusual for Quakers to carry their own warrants, unaccompanied by constables or others, which were to consign them to a prison.

But it was not only in matters which related to the laws of the land, where the early Quakers held their words and engagements sacred. This trait was remarked to be true of them in their concerns in trade. On their first appearance as a society, they suffered as tradesmen, because others, displeased with the peculiarity of their manners, withdrew their custom from their shops. But in a little time, the great outcry against them was, that they got the trade of the country into their hands. This outcry arose in part from a strict execution of all commercial appointments and agreements between them and others, and because they never asked two prices for the commodities which they sold. And the same character attaches to them as a commercial body, though there may be individual exceptions, at the present day.

Neither has this trait been confined to them as the inhabitants of their own country. They have carried it with them wherever they have gone. The treaty of William Penn was never violated. And the estimation, which the Indians put upon the word of this great man and his companions, continues to be put by them upon that of the modern Quakers in America, so that they now come in deputations, out of their own settlements, to consult them on important occasions.

The existence of this trait is probable both from general and from particular considerations.

If, for example, any number of principles should have acted so forcibly and in such a manner upon individuals, as to have procured for them as a body the reputation of a moral people, they must have produced in them a disposition to keep their faith.

[Footnote 37: This character was given by Pliny to the first Christians. They were to avoid fraud, theft, and adultery. They were never to deny any trust, when required to deliver it up, nor to falsify their word on any occasion.]

But the discipline of the Quakers has a direct tendency to produce this feature in their character, and to make it an appendage of Quakerism. For punctuality to words and engagements is a subject of one of the periodical enquiries. It is therefore publicly handed to the notice of the members, as a Christian virtue, that is expected of them, in their public meetings for discipline. And any violation in this respect would be deemed a breach, and cognizable as such, of the Quaker laws.

CHAP. X.

Imperfect traits in the Quaker character—Some of these may be called intellectually defective traits—First imputation of this kind is, that the Quakers are deficient in learning compared with other people—This trait not improbable on account of their devotion to trade—and on account of their controversies and notions about human learning—and of other causes.

The world, while it has given to the Quakers as a body, as it will have now appeared, a more than ordinary share of virtue, has not been without the belief that there are blemishes in their character. What these traits or blemishes are, may be collected partly from books, partly from conversation, and partly from vulgar sayings. They are divisible into two kinds, into intellectually defective, and into morally defective traits; the former relating to the understanding, the latter to the heart.

The first of the intellectually defective traits consists in the imputation, that the Quakers are deficient in the cultivation of the intellect of their children, or that, when they grow up in life, they are found to have less knowledge than others in the higher branches of learning. By this I mean, that they are understood to have but a moderate classical education, to know but little of the different branches of philosophy, and to have, upon the whole, less variety of knowledge than others of their countrymen in the corresponding stations of life.

This trait seems to have originated with the world in two supposed facts. The first is, that there has never been any literary writer of eminence born in the society, Penn, Barclay and others having come into it by convincement, and brought their learning with them. The second is, that the society has never yet furnished a philosopher, or produced any material discovery. It is rather a common remark, that if the education of others had been as limited as that of the Quaker, we should have been probably at this day without a Newton, and might have been strangers to those great discoveries, whether of the art of navigation, or of the circulation of the blood, or of any other kind, which have proved so eminently useful to the comfort, health, and safety of many of the human race.

This trait will be true, or it will be false, as it is applied to the different classes, which may be found in the society of the Quakers. The poor, who belong to it, are all taught to read, and are therefore better educated than the poor belonging to other bodies of men. They who spring from parents whose situation does not entitle them to rank with the middle class, but yet keeps them out of the former, are generally educated, by the help of a subscription, at Ackworth school, and may be said to have more school learning than others in a similar situation in life. The rest, whatever may be their situation, are educated wholly at the expence of their parents, who send them either to private Quaker seminaries, or to schools in the neighbourhood, as they judge it to be convenient or proper. It is upon this body of the Quakers that the imputation can only fall; and as far as these are concerned, I think it may be said with truth, that they possess a less portion of what is usually called liberal knowledge than others in a corresponding station in life. There may be here and there a good classical, or a good mathematical scholar. But in general there are but few Quakers, who excel in these branches of learning. I ought, however, to add, that this character is not likely to remain long with the society. For the young Quakers of the present day seem to me to be sensible of the inferiority of their own education, and to be making an attempt towards the improvement of their minds, by engaging in those, which are the most entertaining, instructive, and useful, I mean, philosophical pursuits.

[Footnote 38: Their parents pay a small annual sum towards their board and clothing. The rest is made up by a subscription among the society, and by the funds of the school.]

That deficiency in literature and science is likely to be a trait in the character of the Quakers, we may pronounce, if we take into consideration circumstances which have happened, and notions which have prevailed, in this society.

The Quakers, like the Jews of old, whether they be rich or poor, are brought up, in obedience to their own laws, to some employment. They are called of course at an early age from their books. It cannot therefore be expected of them, that they should possess the same literary character as those who spend years at our universities, or whose time is not taken up by the concerns of trade.

It happens also in this society, that persons of the poor and middle classes are frequently through industry becoming rich. While these were gaining but a moderate support, they gave their children but a moderate education. But when they came into possession of a greater substance, their children had finished their education, having grown up to men.

The ancient controversy too, relative to the necessity of human learning as a qualification for ministers of the Gospel, has been detrimental to the promotion of literature and science among the Quakers. This controversy was maintained with great warmth and obstinacy on both sides, that is, by the early Quakers, who were men of learning, on the one hand, and by the divines of our universities on the other. The less learned in the society, who read this controversy, did not make the proper distinction concerning it.

They were so interested in keeping up the doctrine, that learning was not necessary for the priesthood, that they seemed to have forgotten that it was necessary at all. Hence knowledge began to be cried down in the society; and though the proposition was always meant to be true with respect to the priesthood only, yet many mistook or confounded its meaning, so that they gave their children but a limited education on that account.

The opinions also of the Quakers relative to classical authors, have been another cause of impeding in some degree their progress in learning, that is, in the classical part of it. They believe these to have inculcated a system of morality frequently repugnant to that of the Christian religion. And the Heathen mythology, which is connected with their writings, and which is fabulous throughout, they conceive to have disseminated romantic notions among youth, and to have made them familiar with fictions, to the prejudice of an unshaken devotedness to the love of truth.

CHAP. XI.

Second trait is, that they are a superstitious people—Circumstances that have given birth to this trait—Quakerism, where it is understood, is seldom chargeable with superstition—Where it is misunderstood, it leads to it—Subjects in which it may be misunderstood are those of the province of the Spirit—and of dress and language—Evils to be misapprehended from a misunderstanding of the former subject.

It may seem wonderful at first sight, that persons, who have discarded an undue veneration for the saints, and the saints days, and the relics of the Roman Catholic religion, who have had the resolution to reject the ceremonials of Protestants, such as baptism and the sacrament of the supper, and who have broken the terrors of the dominion of the priesthood, should, of all others, be chargeable with superstition. But so it is. The world has certainly fixed upon them the character of a superstitious people. Under this epithet much is included. It is understood that Quakers are more ready than others to receive mystical doctrines, more apt to believe in marvellous appearances more willing to place virtue in circumstances, where many would place imposition; and that, independently of all this, they are more scrupulous with respect to the propriety of their ordinary movements, waiting for religious impulses, when no such impulses are expected by other religious people.

This trait of superstition is an ancient trait in the character of the Quakers, and has arisen from the following causes.

It has been long imagined, that where a people devote themselves so exclusively to the influence of the Spirit as the Quakers appear to do, they will not be sufficiently on their guard to make the proper distinctions between imagination and revelation, and that they will be apt to confound impressions, and to bring the divine Spirit out of its proper sphere into the ordinary occurrences of their lives. And in this opinion the world considers itself to have been confirmed by an expression said to have been long in use among Quakers, which is, "that they will do such and such things if they have liberty to do them." Now by this expression the Quakers may mean only, that all human things are so uncertain, and so many unforeseen events may happen, that they dare make no promises, but they will do the things in question if no obstacle should arise to prevent them. And this caution in language runs through the whole society; for they seldom promise but provisionally in any case. But the world has interpreted the expression differently, and maintains that the Quakers mean by it, that they will do such and such things, if they feel that they have liberty or permission from the Spirit of God.

Two other circumstances, which have given birth to this trait in the character of the Quakers, are the singularities of their dress and language. For when they are spoken of by the world, they are usually mentioned under the name of the idolatry or superstition of the Quaker language, or the idolatry or superstition of the Quaker dress.

Now this trait, which has originated in the three causes that have been mentioned, is considered by the world to have been still more confirmed by a circumstance which happened but a few years ago, namely, that when animal magnetism was in fashion, there were more of this society worked upon by these delusions, than of any other.

With respect to the truth of this trait, I believe it cannot easily be made out, as for as animal magnetism is concerned. For though undoubtedly there were Quakers so superstitious as to be led away on this occasion, yet they were very few in number, and not more in proportion than others of other religious denominations. The conduct of these was also considered as reprehensible by the society at large, and some pains were taken to convince them of their error, and of the unsuitableness of such doctrines with the religion they professed.

With respect to the truth of this trait, as it may have existed on other occasions, it may be laid down as a position generally true, that where Quakers understand their own constitution, it can have no place among them. But where they do not understand it, there are few people among whom it is more likely to exist, as we may see from the following account.

It is the doctrine of Quakerism on the subject of the Spirit, that it is an infallible guide to men in their spiritual concerns. But I do not see where it is asserted by any of the Quaker writers, that it is to be a guide to man in all the temporal concerns of his life, or that he is to depreciate the value of human reason. George Fox was very apprehensive that even in matters of religion, which constitute the immediate province of the divine Spirit, men might mistake their own enthusiastic feelings for revelation; and he censured some, to use his own expression, "for having gone out into imaginations." The society also have been apprehensive of the same consequences. Hence one among other reasons for the institution of the office of elders. It is the duty of these to watch over the doctrine of the ministers to see that they preach soundly, and that they do not mistake their own imaginations for the Spirit of God, and mix his wisdom with the waywardness of their own wills. They therefore, who believe in the doctrine of the agency of the Spirit, and at the same time in the necessity of great caution and watchfulness that they may not confound its operations with that of their own fancies, will never incur the charge, which has been brought against the body at large. But if there are others, on the other hand, who give themselves up to this agency without the necessary caution, they will gradually mix their impressions, and will, in time, refer most of them to the same source. They will bring the Divine Being by degrees out of his spiritual province, and introduce him into all the trivial and worthless concerns of their lives. Hence a belief will arise, which cannot fail of binding their minds in the chains of delusion and superstition.

It is the doctrine of Quakerism again on the subject of dress, that plainness and simplicity are required of those who profess the Christian character; that any deviation from these is unwarrantable, if it be made on the plea of conformity to the fashions of the world; that such deviation bespeaks the beginning of an unstable mind; and, if not noticed, may lead into many evils. They therefore, who consider dress in this point of view, will never fall into any errors of mind in their contemplation of this subject. But if there are members, on the other hand, who place virtue in the colour and shape of their cloathing, as some of the Jews did in the broad phylacteries on their garments, they will place it in lifeless appearances and forms, and bring their minds under vassalage to a false religion. And in the same manner it may be observed with respect to language, that if persons in the society lay an undue stress upon it, that is, if they believe truth or falsehood to exist inherently in lifeless words, and this contrary to the sense in which they know they will be understood by the world, so that they dare not pronounce them for religion's sake, they will be in danger of placing religion where it is not, and of falling into errors concerning it, which will be denominated superstition by the world.

As I am now on the subject of superstition, as capable of arising from the three causes that have been mentioned, I shall dwell for a short time on some of the evils which may arise from one of them, or from a misunderstanding of the doctrine of the agency of the Spirit.

I believe it possible, in the first place, for those who receive this doctrine without the proper limitations, that is, for those who attribute every thing exclusively to the Spirit of God, and who draw no line between revelation and the suggestions of their own will, to be guilty of evil actions and to make the Divine Being the author of them all.

I have no doubt, for example, that many of those, who engaged in the crusades, considered themselves as led into them by the Spirit of God. But what true Quaker, in these days, would wish to make the Almighty the author of all the bloodshed in the wars that were undertaken on this account?

The same may be said with respect to martyrdoms. For there is reason to believe, that many who were instrumental in shedding the blood of their fellow-creatures, because they happened to differ from them in religious opinion, conceived that they were actuated by the divine Spirit, and that they were doing God service, and aiding the cause of religion by their conduct on such occasions. But what true Quaker would believe that the Father of justice and mercy was the author of these bloody persecutions, or that, if men were now to feel an impulse in their own minds to any particular action, they ought to obey it, if it were to lead them to do evil that good might come?

The same may be said with respect to many of the bad laws, which are to be found in the codes of the different nations of the world. Legislators no doubt have often thought themselves spiritually guided when they made them. And judges, who have been remarkable for appealing to the divine Spirit in the course of their lives, have made no hesitation to execute them. This was particularly the case with Sir Matthew Hale. If there be any one, whose writings speak a more than ordinary belief in the agency of the Spirit of God, it is this great and estimable man. This spirit he consulted not only in the spiritual, but in the temporal concerns, of his life. And yet he sentenced to death a number of persons, because they were reputed to be witches. But what true Quaker believes in witchcraft? or does he not rather believe, that the Spirit of God, it rightly understood, would have protested against condemnation for a crime, which does not exist?

But the mischief, if a proper distinction be not made between the agency of the Spirit and that of the will of man, may spread farther, and may reach the man himself, and become injurious both to his health, his intellect, and his usefulness, and the Divine Being may be made again the author of it all.

Many, we all know, notwithstanding their care and attention, have found that they have gone wrong in their affairs in various instances of their lives, that is, events have shewn that they have taken a wrong course. But if there be those who suppose themselves in these instances to have been acted upon by the Spirit or God, what is more likely than that they may imagine that they have lost his favour, and that looking upon themselves as driven by him into the wrong road, they may fall into the belief, that they are among the condemned reprobate, and pine away, deprived of their senses, in a state of irretrievable misery and despair?

Others again may injure their health, and diminish their comfort and their utility in another way. And here I may remark, that if I have seen what the world would call superstition among the Quakers, it has been confined principally to a few females, upon whose constitution, more delicate than that of men, an attention to undistinguished impressions, brought on in a course of time by a gradual depreciation of human reason, has acted with considerable force. I fear that some of these, in the upright intention of their hearts to consult the Almighty on all occasions as the sole arbiter of every thing that is good, have fostered their own infirmities, and gone into retirements so frequent, as to have occasioned these to interfere with the duties of domestic comfort and social good, and that they have been at last so perplexed with doubts and an increasing multitude of scruples, that they have been afraid of doing many things, because they have not had a revelation for them. The state of such worthy persons is much to be pitied. What must be their feelings under such a conflict, when they are deserted by human reason? What an effect will not such religious doubts and perplexities have upon their health? What impediments do they not throw in the way of their own utility?

I should be sorry if by any observations, such as the preceding, I should be thought to censure any one for the morality of his feelings. And still more sorry should I be, if I were to be thought to have any intention of derogating from the character of the Supreme Being. I am far from denying his omniscience, for I believe that he sees every sparrow that falls to the ground, and even more, that he knows the innermost thoughts of men. I deny not his omnipresence, for I believe that he may be seen in all his works. I deny neither his general nor his particular providence, nor his hearing of our prayers, nor his right direction in our spiritual concerns, nor his making of all things work together for good to those who love him. Neither do I refuse to admit him either into our journies, or into our walks, or into our chambers, for he can make all the things we see subservient to our moral instruction, and his own glory. But I should be sorry to have him considered as a clock, that is to inform us about the times of our ordinary movements, or to make him a prompter in all our worldly concerns, or to oblige him to take his seat in animal magnetism, or to reside in the midst marvellous delusions. Why should we expect a revelation in the most trivial concerns of our lives, where our reason will inform us? Why, like the waggoner, apply to Jupiter, when we may remove the difficulty by putting our own shoulders to the wheels? If we are reasonable creatures, we can generally tell, whether we ought to go forwards or backwards, or to begin, or to postpone, whether our actions are likely to be innocent or hurtful, or whether we are going on an errand of benevolence or of evil. In fact, there can be no necessity for this constant appeal to the Spirit in all our worldly concerns, while we possess our reason as men. And unless some distinction be made between the real agency of God and our own volitions, which distinction true Quakerism suggests, we shall be liable to be tossed to and fro by every wind that blows, and to become the creatures of a superstition, that may lead us into great public evils, while it may be injurious to our health and intellect, and to the happiness and utility of our lives.

CHAP. XII.

Morally defective traits—First of these is that of obstinacy—This was attached also to the early Christians—No just foundation for the existence of this trait.

I come now to the consideration of those which I have denominated morally defective traits.

The first trait of this kind, which is attached to the character of the Quakers, is that of an obstinate spirit.

This trait is a very ancient one. It was observed in the time of George Fox, of the members of this society, that they were as "stiff as trees," and this idea concerning them has come down to the present day.

The origin of this trait must be obvious to all. The Quakers, as we have seen, will neither pay tithes, nor perform military service, nor illuminate their houses, like other people, though they are sure of suffering by their refusal to comply with custom in these cases. Now, when individuals, few in number, become singular, and differ from the world at large, it is generally considered that the majority are in the right, and that the minority are in the wrong. But obstinacy may be defined to be a perseverance in that which is generally considered to be wrong.

This epithet has attached, and will attach to those who resist the popular opinion, till men are better educated, or till they lose their prejudices, or have more correct and liberal notions on religion. The early Christians were themselves accused of obstinacy, and this even by the enlightened Pliny. He tells, us, that they would not use wine and frankincense before the statues of the emperors; and that "there was no question that for such obstinacy they deserved punishment."

[Footnote 39: "Pervicaciam certe et inflexibitem obstinationem debere puniri."]

In judging of the truth of this trait, two queries will arise. First, whether the Quakers, in adhering rigidly to those singularities which have produced it, are really wrong as a body of Christians? And, secondly, whether they do not conscientiously believe themselves to be right?

In the case of the early Christians, which has been mentioned, we, who live at this day, have no doubt that Pliny put a false estimate on their character. We believe them to have done their duty, and we believe also that they considered themselves as doing it, when they refused divine honours to the emperors. And the action, therefore, which Pliny denominated obstinacy, would, if it had been left to us to name it, have been called inflexible virtue, as arising out of a sense of the obligations imposed upon them by the Christian religion.

In the same manner we may argue with respect to the Quakers. Who, for example, if he will try to divest himself of the prejudices of custom, and of the policy of the world, feels such a consciousness of his own powers as positively to pronounce, that the notions of the Quakers are utterly false, as to the illicitness of wars under the Christian system? The arguments of the Quakers on this subject are quite as good, in my apprehension, as any that I have heard advanced on the other side of the question. These arguments too are unquestionably much more honourable to Christianity, and much more consistent with the nature and design of the Gospel dispensation. They are supported also by the belief and the practice of the earliest Christians. They are arguments again, which have suggested themselves to many good men, who were not Quakers, and which have occasioned doubts in some instances, and conviction in others, against the prejudice of education and the dominion of custom. And if the event should ever come to pass, which most Christians expect, that men will one day or other turn their swords and their spears into ploughshares and pruning-hooks, they, who live in that day, will applaud the perseverance of the Quakers in this case, and weep over the obstinacy and inconsistency of those who combated their opinions.

But the great question after all is, whether the Quakers believe themselves in this or in any other of their religious scruples, to be right, as a Christian body? If there are those among them who do not, they give into the customs of the world, and either leave the society themselves, or become disowned. It is therefore only a fair and a just presumption, that all those who continue in the society, and who keep up to these scruples to the detriment of their worldly interest, believe themselves to be right. But this belief of their own rectitude, even if they should happen to be wrong, is religion to them, and ought to be estimated so by us in matters in which an interpretation of Gospel principles is concerned. This is but an homage due to conscience, after all the blood that has been shed in the course of Christian persecutions, and after all the religious light that has been diffused among us since the reformation of our religion.

CHAP. XIII.

SECT. I.

Next trait is that of a money-getting spirit—Probability of the truth of this trait examined—An undue eagerness after money not unlikely to be often the result of the frugal and commercial habits of the society—but not to the extent, as insisted on by the world—This eagerness, wherever it exists, seldom chargeable with avarice.

The next trait in the character of the Quakers is that of a money-getting spirit, or of a devotedness to the acquisition of money in their several callings and concerns.

This character is considered as belonging so generally to the individuals of this society, that it is held by the world to be almost inseparable from Quakerism. A certain writer has remarked, that they follow their concerns in pursuit of riches, "with a step as steady as time, and with an appetite as keen as death."

I do not know what circumstances have given birth to this trait. That the Quakers are a thriving body we know. That they may also appear, when known to be a domestic people, and to have discarded the amusements of the world, to be more in their shops and counting-houses than others, is probable. And it is not unlikely, that, in consequence of this appearance, connected with this worldly prosperity, they may be thought to be more intent than others upon the promotion of their pecuniary concerns. There are circumstances, however, belonging to the character and customs of the society, which would lead to an opposite conclusion. The Quakers, in the first place, are acknowledged to be a charitable people. But if so, they ought not to be charged, at least, with that species of the money-getting spirit, which amounts to avarice. It is also an undoubted fact, that they give up no small portion of their time, and put themselves to no small expence, on account of their religion. In country places they allot one morning in the week, and in the towns generally two, besides the Sunday, to their religious worship. They have also their monthly meetings, and after these their quarterly, to attend, on account of their discipline. And this they do frequently at a great distance, and after a considerable absence as tradesmen, from their homes. I do not mean to insinuate by this latter instance, that men become pious, and therefore proof against the influence of money, exactly in proportion as they attend their religious meetings, but that, where they are voraciously intent upon the getting of money, they could hardly be expected to make such a sacrifice of their time.

But whatever may be the appearance on either side, the question is, whether the imputation of the trait, which is now under our consideration, be founded in fact. What circumstances make in favour of it? What circumstances make against it? And which of these preponderate on the whole?

We may say then, at the first sight, that the precepts of Quakerism make decidedly against it. And we may say again, that it ought to be expected, that all those principles and circumstances, which have an influence in the production of moral character, or of such a character as belongs to the Quakers as a body, should work together either towards its prevention or its cure.

On the other hand, if we examine the situation of the society, we shall find circumstances, the operation of which is directly in favour of such a trait.

And first, in looking into the human heart, we seem to discover a circumstance, which, on account of the situation alluded to, may operate as a spring in producing it. Men, generally speaking, love consequence. Now the Quakers, though they have consequence in their own society, have none in the world. They can be neither legislators nor magistrates. They can take no titles to distinguish them. They pass therefore in the world, like the common and undistinguished herd, except from the circumstances of their dress. But riches give all men consequence. And it is not clear to me, but that this circumstance may have its operation on the minds of some who are called Quakers, in contributing to the production of the money-getting spirit, inasmuch as it may procure them a portion of estimation, which they cannot otherwise have, while they remain in their own body.

In looking again into the human heart, we find another, and this a powerful spring, connected with the situation of the society, for the production of such a trait.

The Quakers, as I have observed before, are mostly in trade. Now they are generally a sedate, thoughtful, sober, diligent, and honest people. It is not then too much to say, with these qualifications, that they will be as successful in trade as others. Hence their incomes will be as great, in proportion to their capitals, as those of others, from the same source.

But let us look for a moment at their outgoings. They neither spend nor lose their money at cards, or at horse-races, or by any other species of gaming. They do not waste their substance either in drinking at taverns or at home. Not having, in general, an enlarged education, or a taste for literature, they have no expensive libraries. They buy no costly paintings. They neither powder their hair, nor dress in a splendid manner. They use no extravagant furniture. They keep no packs of hounds for their diversion.

They are never seen at the theatres. They have neither routes, balls, nor music meetings. They have neither expensive liveries nor equipages. Hence it must follow, that their outgoings, as far as their living is concerned, cannot in general be as great as those of others in a similar condition of life. But if their inlets are greater than their outlets of money, when compared with those of other persons, a greater overplus of money beyond the expences of living, will be the constant result, or there will be a greater increasing accumulation of money, upon the whole, than falls within the possession of others. Now a question arises here, founded on a knowledge of the infirmity of our nature. Are men likely, in general, constituted as they are, to see the golden idol constantly rising in dimensions before them, and to refrain front worshipping it, or, are they likely to see it without a corruption of their moral vision? It is observed by one of the scriptural writers, "A merchant shall hardly keep himself from doing wrong, and a huckster shall not be free from sin." And where is it, that this old saying, except the mind be strongly fortified by religion, will not be found equally true in the present, as in former times? The truth is, that the old maxim, Creseit amor nummi quantum ipsa pecunia creseit, is a just one. That is, it is true, "that the coming in of money in an undue proportion begets the love of it", that the love of money again leads to the getting of more; that the getting of more again generally increases the former love. And hence a round is kept up of circumstances and feelings, till a money-getting spirit creeps into the character of him, who is placed in a situation so unfortunate for the purity of his heart.

[Footnote 40: Ecclesiasticus xxvi. 29.]

These then are the acting and the counteracting circumstances on both sides. Which of the two are likely to be predominant, we must conjecture. When men have become full grown Quakers, the latter will lose their power. But where they have not (and it is to be presumed that there are many in the society who have not reached this stature, and many again who bear only the name of their profession) they will frequently prevail. I own I fear that precepts, though there may be a general moral bias, will not always be found successful against those, which are considered to be the most powerful of the temptations, to which our nature is exposed. I own, when I consider that the Quakers, in consequence of their commercial and frugal habits, have greater pecuniary accumulations before their eyes than others in a similar condition of life, when I consider how few are able to bear these accumulations without moral injury to themselves, and that even the early Christians began to relax in their character when they begun to be prosperous, I am of opinion, that there is some foundation far the existence of such a spirit, though not to the extent, as insisted on by the world; or, that there is in the society, notwithstanding the many bright and amiable exceptions that are to be found in it, greater eagerness after wealth than is consistent with its religious profession. And to this opinion I am inclined from another consideration, which cannot be overlooked in the present case. The book of Extracts itself acknowledges the existence of such a spirit, for it characterises it under the name of "hastening to be rich," and it calls it "a growing evil."

But when I say that I so for accede to the opinion of the world, as to allow that the money-getting spirit may be fixed upon a part of the society, I feel that I ought to make a proper distinction concerning it. I must observe, that the money-getting spirit, wherever it may be chargeable upon Quakers, seldom belongs to that species which is called avarice. It is by no means incongruous to suppose, that there may be in the same person an unreasonable love of money, and yet a shew of benevolence. The money-getting spirit will have a different effect, as it operates upon different persons. Upon those, who have been brought up in an ignorant and unfeeling manner, it will operate to make them hoard their substance, and to keep it exclusively to themselves. But it will not always hinder those who have been humanely educated, though it may lead them to unreasonable accumulations, from dispensing a portion of their gains. In the first instance it is highly criminal, because it keeps the whole of its talent in a napkin. In the second, though less criminal, it is greatly to be deplored, but more particularly in a Quaker, who, making a higher profession of Christianity than many others, ought to give to the world the example of a purer mind.

SECT. II.

Farther observations on the subject of the former trait—Practicable methods suggested for its extirpation—These methods not destructive, but promotive, of the temporal interests of the members of this society, and consistent with the religion they profess.

As the Quakers appear to me, in consequence of their commercial and frugal habits, to be in danger of contracting a money-getting spirit, and as this spirit is the worst feature that can exist in the Quaker character, I shall allot a few pages to the farther consideration of the subject, with a view of the prevention of such an evil.

That it is the worst feature that can exist in the character of the society, I repeat. It is worse than a want of knowledge, or than superstition, because these relate to the understanding, while this is confined to the heart. It renders the system of the moral education of the Quakers almost nugatory. For what is the use of keeping the mind in a state of spiritual purity by means of prohibitions, or by attempting to shut it out from the knowledge of corruptive amusements, if it be afterwards to be rendered impure by the love of money? It occasions them again to bear their testimony as it were against their own religion. For a Quaker is not in the situation of on ordinary person. He looks upon himself as a highly professing Christian; as one, who is not to conform to the fashions of the world; as one, who is to lead a life of self-denial; as one, who is to go forward in virtue, his belief being that of a possibility of perfection even in the present life. He considers himself too as a representative of the early Christians, and holds himself ready to follow them by the bearing of his testimony, into suffering, and even unto death. But what Christian can harbour a money-getting spirit, or be concerned in an extensive accumulation of wealth? If a Quaker therefore should go into the common road, and fall down before the idol mammon, like any other ordinary person, how can the world give him any pretension but to an ordinary religion?

My object in the present consideration of the subject, will be to shew the Quakers in general, and those in particular who may need it, some practical cure for this evil, and to convince them, that the mode of effecting it will not be detrimental to the temporal interests of their families, but promotive of their spiritual, and consistent with the religion they profess.

The first method, which I would recommend to those who are in trade, and who know their own habits of life, and the extent of their families, would be to fix upon a certain sum, which they may think sufficient for a future decent and moderate competency, and to leave off business, as soon as this should be obtained. Such a step would be useful. It would be making room for others to live as well as themselves. It would be honourable, for it would be generous. And it would operate as a certain preventive of the money-getting spirit, as well as of the imputation of it. For if such a retreat from trade, were laid down and known as a general custom of the society, the Quakers might bid their hearts rise in defiance against the corruptions of money, and their reputation against the clamours of the world.

This step, hard and difficult as it may appear to those who are thriving in the world, is, notwithstanding, not a novel one, if we may judge either by the example of many of the pure minded Christians of other denominations, or by that of many estimable persons in this society. John Woolman, among many others, was uneasy on account of his business "growing cumbersome," for so he expresses it, lest it should hurt the purity of his mind. And he contracted it, leaving himself only enough of it, and this by the labour of his own hands, for a decent support. And here I might mention other individuals of this society, if I had no objection to offend the living by praise, who, following his example, have retired upon only a moderate competency, though in the way of great accumulations, for no other reason than because they were afraid, lest such accumulations should interfere with their duty, or injure their character, as Christians.

But if this measure should not be approved of under an idea that men ought to have employments for their time, or that in these days of increasing taxes and of progressively expensive living, they cannot specify the sum that may be sufficient for their future wants, I have another to propose, in consequence of which they may still follow their commercial pursuits, and avoid the imputation in question. I mean that the Quakers ought to make it a rule, after the annual expences of living have been settled, to lay by but small savings. They ought never to accustom their eyes to behold an undue accumulation of money, but liberally to deal it out in charity to the poor and afflicted in proportion to their gains, thus making their occupations a blessing to mankind. No other measure will be effectual but this, if the former be not resolved upon, while they continue in trade. Their ordinary charity, it is clear, will not do. Large as it may have been, it has not been found large enough to prove a corrective of this spirit in the opinion of the world. Indeed, it matters not how large a charitable donation may seem, if we view it either as a check upon this spirit, or as an act of merit, but how large it is, when compared with the bulk of the savings that are left. A hundred pounds, given away annually in benevolence, may appear something, and may sound handsomely in the ears of the public. But if this sum be taken from the savings of two thousand, it will be little less than a reproach to the donor as a Christian. In short, no other way than the estimation of the gift by the surplus-saving will do in the case in question. But this would certainly be effectual to the end proposed. It would entirely keep down the money-getting spirit. It would also do away the imputation of it in the public mind. For it is impossible in this case, that the word Quakerism should not become synonimous with charity, as it ought to be, if Quakerism be a more than ordinary profession of the Christian religion.

Now these methods are not chimerical, but practicable. There can be no reasonable objection against them, because they allow of the acquisition of a decent and moderate competency. The only one that can be started will be, that Quakers may injure the temporal interests of their children, or that they cannot, upon this plan, leave them independent at their deaths ...

That independence for children is the general aim of the world, I know well. But I know also, in reply to this objection, that Christianity has no such word as independence in her book. For of what do people wish to make their children independent? Certainly not of Providence, for that would be insanity indeed. Of the poor then shall I say? That is impossible, for how could they get their daily bread? Of the rich, then, like themselves? That would be folly, for where would they form their friendships or their connubial connections, in which they must place a portion of the happiness of their lives? Do they wish then to make them independent of society at large, so as not to do it good? That is against all religion. In short it is impossible, while we exist in this life, to be independent one of another. We are bound by Christianity in one great chain, every link of which is to support the next; or the band is broken. But if they mean by independence such a moneyed situation as shall place their children out of the reach of the frowns, and crosses, and vicissitudes of the world, so that no thought or care shall be necessary for the means of their own livelihood, I fear they are procuring a situation for them, which will be injurious even to their temporal interests as men.

The matter then seems to me to be brought to this question, whether it is better, I mean as a general proposition, to bring up children with the expectation of such a moderate portion of wealth, that they shall see the necessity of relying upon their own honest endeavours and the Divine support, or to bring them up with such notions of independence, that, in the pride and exultation of their hearts, they may be induced to count themselves mighty, and to lose sight of the power and providence of God?

If we were to look into the world for an answer to this question, we should find no greater calamity than that of leaving to children an affluent independence. Such persons, when grown up, instead of becoming a blessing, are generally less useful than others. They are frequently proud and haughty, fancying themselves omnipotent, they bid defiance to the opinions of the virtuous part of the community. To the laws of honour and fashion they pay a precise obedience, but trample under foot, as of little consequence, the precepts of the Christian religion. Having sensual gratifications in their power, they indulge to excess. By degrees they ruin their health and fortunes, and get wisdom by experience, when it is too late to use it. How many young persons have I known, and I wish I could make a different statement, whose ruin originated wholly in a sense of their own independence of the world!

Neither, if we look into the society of the Quakers, shall we find a different account. It is undoubtedly true, though there are many amiable exceptions, that the worst examples in it are generally among the children of the rich. These presently take wings, and fly away, so that, falling into the corruptive and destructive fashions of the times, their parents have only been heaping up riches; not knowing who were to gather them. And here it may be remarked, that the Quaker education, by means of its prohibitions, greatly disqualifies its young members, who may desert from the society, from acting prudently afterwards. They will be, in general, but children, and novices in the world. Kept within bounds till this period, what is more probable than that, when they break out of them, they will bunch-into excess. A great river may be kept in its course by paying attention to its banks, but if you make a breach in these restrictive walls, you let it loose, and it deluges the plains below.

In short, whether we turn our eyes to the Quaker society, or to the world at large, we cannot consider an affluent independence as among the temporal advantages of youth. And as they, who only leave their children a moderate portion of substance, so that they shall see the necessity of relying upon their own honest endeavours, and the Divine support, act wisely in their own generation, so they act only consistently with the religion they profess. For what does the religion of the Quakers hold out to them as the best attainment in life? Is it not spiritual knowledge? Is it not that knowledge, which shall fit them best for the service of their Maker? But such knowledge is utterly unattainable while a money-getting spirit exists; for it has been declared by the highest authority, that we cannot serve God and mammon.

CHAP. XIV.

Another trait is that of a want of animation or affection—This an appearance only, and not a reality, arising from a proper subjugation of the passions—from the prohibitions relative to dress—and address—and the amusements of the world.

It is said next of the Quakers, that they are a cold and inanimate people; and that they have neither the ordinary affection, nor the gradation of affection, of other people.

I may immediately pronounce upon this trait, that it is merely an outward appearance. The Quakers have as warm feelings as the rest of their countrymen. Their love of their fellow-creatures, more conspicuous in them than in many others, as has been amply shewn, gives them a claim to the possession of warm and affectionate feeling. The Quakers too have the character of a domestic people; but surely, if they do not possess affection, and this in a very high degree, they must have miserable homes. There is indeed a want of gradation in their affections, which may be traced upon some occasions. In making their wills, for example, they are not apt to raise up an eldest son to the detriment of the rest of their offspring. And this certainly is a proof, that they do not possess the gradation of affection of many other people! Happy is it for their own comfort and the welfare of their families, that they give this proof to the world of this equal affection for their children.

That this trait is only an appearance, and not a reality, I shall shew, by staring many outward circumstances, in the Quaker constitution, which may be preventive of apparent animation, but which can have no influence on the heart.

We must all of us be sensible, that both opinions and customs have an influence on the warmth or coldness of our characters. Who would expect, if two faithful portraits could have been handed down to us from antiquity, to find the same gravity or coldness of countenance and manners in an Athenian, as in a Spartan? And in the same manner who can expect, that there will not be a difference in the appearance of Quakers and other people?

The truth is, that the discipline and education of the Quakers produce an appearance of a want of animation, and this outward appearance the world has falsely taken as a symbol of the character of the heart. Can we expect that a due subjugation of the passions, which is insisted upon in true Quaker families, will give either warmth to the countenance, or spirit to the outward manners? Do not the passions animate, and give a tone to the characters of men? Can we see then the same variety of expression in the faces of the Quakers as in those of others on this account? The actions of men, again, enliven their outward appearances, but Quakers, being forbidden to use the address of the world, can assume no variety of action in their intercourse with others. The amusements, again, of the world, such as of music and the theatre, reach the mind, and, animating it, give a greater expression to the countenance, on which the contemplation afterwards produces a similar though a slighter effect. But in what Quakers can you see sensibility from the same cause? The dress too, of the members of this society gives them an appearance of gravity and dulness. It makes them also shy of their fellow citizens. But gravity, and dulness, and shyness, have generally, each of them, the appearance of coldness of manners.

CHAP. XV.

Another trait is that of evasiveness in speech—This an appearance only, arising from a peculiar regard to truth—and from a caution about the proper use of words, induced by circumstances in the discipline, and by the peculiarities in the Quaker language.

It is alleged against the Quakers, as another bad trait in their character, that they are not plain and direct, but that they are evasive in their answers to any questions that may be asked them.

There is no doubt but that the world, who know scarcely any thing about the Quakers, will have some reason, if they judge from their outward manner of expression, to come to such a conclusion. There is often a sort of hesitation in their speech, which has the appearance of evasiveness. But though there may be such an appearance, their answers to questions are full and accurate when finally given; and unquestionably there is no intention in them either to hold back any thing, or to deceive.

This outward appearance, strange to relate, arises in part from an amiable trait in the character of the Quakers!! Their great desire to speak the truth, and not to exceed it, occasions often a sort of doubtfulness of speech. It occasions them also, instead of answering a question immediately, to ask other questions, that they may see the true bearings of the thing intended to be known. The same appearance of doubt runs also through the whole society in all those words which relate to promises, from the same cause. For the Quakers, knowing the uncertainty of all human things, and the impossibility of fulfilling but provisionally, seldom, as I have observed before, promise any thing positively, that they may not come short of the truth. The desire therefore of uttering the truth has in part brought this accusation upon their heads.

Other circumstances also to be found within the Quaker constitution have a tendency to produce the same effect.

In their monthly and quarterly and annual meetings for discipline, they are taught by custom to watch the propriety of the expressions that are used in the wording of their minutes, that these may accurately represent the sense of the persons present. And this habit of caution about the use of words in the affairs of their own society naturally begets a caution concerning it also in their intercourse with the world.

The peculiarities of their language produce also a similar circumspection. For where people are restrained from the use of expressions which are gene rally adopted by others, and this in the belief that, as a highly professing people, they ought to be watchful over their words as well as their actions, a sort of hesitation will accompany them, or a sort of pause will be perceptible, while they are choosing as it were the proper words for a reply to any of the questions that may be asked them.

CHAP. XVI.

Another trait is that of shyness—This an appearance only, arising from the former trait—and from that of coldness of manners—and from the great sobriety of the Quaker character.

Another bad trait, which the world has fixed upon the Quakers, is that of being a sly people. This trait has been long given them. We find it noticed by Pope:

"The Quaker sly, the Presbyterian sour."

This charge is grounded on appearances. It arises in part from the last mentioned trait in their character; for if men be thought cautious in the use of their words, and evasive in their answers, whether they be so or not, they will be marked as sly.

It arises again from the trait of want of animation or of coldness of manners. For if men of good understanding, in consequence of the subjugation of their passions, appear always to be cool, they will have an appearance of wariness.

It arises again from the great sobriety of the Quakers. For where men are always sober, they appear to be always on their guard, and men, who are always on their guard, are reputed cunning.

These circumstances of coolness and sobriety, when called into action, will only confirm the world in the opinion of the existence of the trait in question. For it will not be easy to deceive a man of but moderate understanding, who never loses his senses either by intoxication or by passion. And what man, in such habits, will not make a better bargain than one who is hot in his temper, or who is accustomed to be intoxicated?

Hence the trait arises from appearances, which are the result of circumstances, favourable to the morality of the Quaker character.

CHAP. XVII.

Last bad trait is a disregard of truth—Apparent rise of this trait—Falsehood of it probable from considerations on the language of the Quakers—from their prohibition of detraction—their rejection of romantic books—their punctuality to words and engagements—and their ideas with respect to the unlawfulness of civil oaths.

The last charge against the Quakers will be seen in a vulgar expression, which should have had no place in this book, if it had not been a saying in almost every body's mouth. The expression, is, "Though they will not swear, they will lie."

This trait has arisen in part from those different circumstances, which have produced the appearance of evasiveness. For if people are thought evasive, they will always be thought liars. Evasiveness and lying are almost synonimous terms. It is not impossible also, if Quakers should appear to give a doubtful answer, that persons may draw false conclusions from thence, and therefore may suppose them to have spoken falsely. These two circumstances of an apparent evasiveness, and probably of a deduction of conclusions from doubtful or imaginary premises, have, I apprehend, produced an appearance, which the world has interpreted into evil.

No trait, however, can be more false than this. I know of no people, who regard truth more than the Quakers. Their whole system bends and directs to truth. One of the peculiarities of their language, or their rejection of many of the words which other people use, because they consider them as not religiously appropriate to the objects of which they are the symbols, serves as a constant admonition to them to speak the truth.

Their prohibition of all slanderous reports, as mentioned in a former volume, has a tendency to produce the same effect; for detraction is forbidden partly on the idea, that all such rumours on character may be false.

They reject also the reading of plays and novels, partly under a notion, that the subjects and circumstances in these are fictitious, and that a taste therefore, for the reading, of these, if acquired, might familiarize their youth with fictions, and produce in them a romantic and lying spirit.

It is a trait, again, in the character of the Quakers, as we have seen, that they are remarkable for their punctuality in the performance of their words and engagements. But such punctuality implies neither more nor less, than that the words spoken by Quakers are generally fulfilled; and, if they are generally fulfilled, then the inference is, that all such words have been generally truths.

To this I may add, that the notions of the Quakers on the subject of oaths, and their ideas of the character which it becomes them to sustain in life, must have a powerful effect upon them in inducing an attention to the truth; for they consider Jesus Christ to have abolished civil oaths, because he wished to introduce a more excellent system than that of old, that is, because he meant it to be understood by his disciples, that he laid such an eternal obligation upon them to speak truth, that oaths were to be rendered unnecessary, where persons make a profession of his religion.

CHAP. XVIII.

SECT. I.

Character of the Quaker women—This differs a little from that of the men—Women share in the virtues of the former—but do not always partake of all their reputed imperfections—are not chargeable with a want of knowledge—nor with the money-getting spirit—Modesty a feature in their character.

Having now amply enquired into the character of the men, I shall say a few words on the subject of that of the women of this society. For though it might be supposed at the first sight (the Quakers being cast as it were in one mould) that the same character would attach to both, yet it must be obvious, on farther consideration, that it cannot be wholly applicable to the female sex.

It may be laid down as a position, that the women of this society share in the virtues of the men. They possess their benevolence, their independence of mind, and the other good traits in their moral character. But they do not always partake of all their reputed imperfections.

The want of knowledge, which was reckoned among the failings of the men, can have no room as a charge against the women.

For, first, let us compare the Quaker women with the Quaker men. Now it generally happens in the world, that men have more literary knowledge than women, but this is not so generally the case in this society. As the women here are not taken from their books, like the men, at an early age, and put into trade, they have no bar, like these, to the farther improvement of their minds. They advance often in the acquisition of knowledge, while the latter, in consequence of their attention to business, are kept stationary. Hence it almost uniformly happens, that they are quite as well informed, and that they have as great a variety of knowledge as these, so that they suffer no disparagement, as the women of the world do, by a comparison with the other sex.

Neither will the Quaker women be considered as deficient in knowledge, if compared with women of other religious denominations. It is too much the practice, but particularly in the higher circles, to educate females for shew. We too seldom see a knowledge of the domestic duties. To dance well, to sing well, and to play well, these are the usual accomplishments that are insisted on, and they are insisted upon with an earnestness, as if they included all the valuable purposes of life. Thus the best part of youth is spent in the acquirement of trivial things: or rather the acquirement of such things takes up so much time, as to leave but little for the moral and intellectual improvement of the mind. The great object, on the other hand, of the education of the Quaker females, is utility and not shew. They are taught domestic economy, or the cares and employments of a house. They are taught to become good wives and good mothers. Prohibited the attainments of music and dancing, and many of the corruptive amusements of the world, they have ample time for the improvement of the understanding. Thus they have in general as good an education as other females, as far as literary acquirements are concerned; so that, whether they are compared with Quaker men, or with the other women of the island, they will not incur the imputation of a deficiency of knowledge.

It must be obvious too, that the money-getting spirit, which the world has fixed upon as a trait in the character of some of the men, can seldom be a trait in that of the women of this society. For men are the principals in trade. They lay their plans for the getting of money. They see the accumulating surplus rise. They handle it. They count it. They remember it. The women, on the other hand, see it only in the disposition of their husbands or parents, who make probably a larger allowance for domestic wants or gratifications than before. Hence a charge cannot be so frequently brought against them of a want of that spiritual mindedness, which is the great characteristic of Quakerism, as they have but little to do with the mammon of the world.

To these exceptions in Quaker women from the reputed imperfections of Quaker men, I cannot help adding in this place, that the females of this society are peculiarly distinguishable for that which has been at all times considered as one of the brightest ornaments of their sex. Modesty is particularly conspicuous in their looks and in their whole outward demeanour. It is conspicuous in their conversation. It is conspicuous also in their dress. And here it may not be improper to observe, that, whatever objections may be made to the Quaker apparel, it is estimable, as far as it gives this appearance of modesty to the females who wear it, or rather as far as it hinders them from wearing the loose and indelicate garments, which are frequently worn, without any scruple, by many of the females of the world.

SECT. II.

Quaker women, besides their private, have a public character—Low light in which women have been held—Importance given them by chivalry—and by the revival of learning in Europe—and by the introduction of Christianity—but still held in an inferior light—Quakers have given them their due importance in society—Influence of their public character on their minds.

The Quaker women, independently of their private, have that which no other body of women have, a public character. This is a new era in female history. I shall therefore make a few observations on this, before I proceed to another subject.

It is melancholy, when we look into the history of women, to see the low estimation in which they have been held from the earliest times. It is possible, because they have not possessed the strength of constitution, that they may have been thought not to have had the intellect of men. It is possible, because domestic cares and the rearing of children have been consigned to them, that other occupations may not have been considered as falling within the province of their stations. But whatever may have been the causes, polygamy or concubinage has unquestionably been the greatest, in hindering women from occupying an useful, dignified, and important station in society. This custom has held them up as little better than slaves, or than living toys or play-things. And this custom has prevailed over a great portion of the globe from times of the earliest antiquity to the present day.

Among the many circumstances which contributed to give importance to women in Europe, we may reckon the introduction of chivalry. Honour and humanity were the characteristics of this institution. Hence weakness was to be protected by it. And as weakness was more particularly the lot of women, so these became more peculiarly the objects of its care. Hence women began to feel a consequence, which had been hitherto denied them. They were treated with politeness and tenderness by all, and men began to be even solicitous of their applause. But though this was the case, chivalry did not elevate them beyond a certain height. It rendered a polite attention to them essential. But this attention was an homage to the weakness of females, and not to their intellect. It presupposed no capacity of usefulness in them, for every thing, in fact, was to be done for them, and they were to do but little for themselves.

The revival of learning in the twelfth century was another cause of adding to the importance of women. As men became more learned, they began to respect the power of the human understanding. They began to be acquainted, by means of history, with the talents of women in former ages. They began to give a better education to their families. These circumstances produced a more enlarged opinion of female genius. Hence learning became an instrument of giving new consequence to women. But it gave it to them on a principle different from that of chivalry: for whereas chivalry insisted upon a polite attention to them on account of the weakness of their constitutions, learning insisted upon it on account of the strength of their understanding, or because they were intellectual and reasonable beings. But that which contributed most to make women important in society, was the introduction of the Christian religion. By the mild spirit which it diffused, it produced a certain suavity of behaviour towards them. By the abolition of polygamy it allowed of no division of a man's love among many women, but limited it to one. Thus it made one woman dearer than another, and of course every individual woman of consequence. By the abolition of polygamy, it added to their consequence again, by raising them from the rank of slaves to that of the companions of men. This importance it increased again by the inculcation of specific duties towards them, and by the doctrine, that, as all, without exception, were equally accountable for their actions, and the Divine Being was no respecter of persons, so all, whether men or women, were of equal importance in his sight.

But though Christianity has operated, as it always will, where it is felt in the heart, to the production of a tender attention to women, and to the procuring of an honourable station for them in society, we have yet to lament, that this operation has not been more general, considering our public profession of this religion, than we find it at the present day. Women are still seldom appreciated as they ought to be. They are still weighed in a different scale from men. Their education is still limited, as if their understandings, notwithstanding the honourable testimony which history has borne concerning them, were incapable of high attainments. If homage be paid to their beauty, very little is paid to their opinions. Limits also are assigned to the sphere of their utility. To engage in other pursuits than they do would be thought strange. In short, the education they receive marks the inferior situation for which they are considered to be designed. Its tendency is mostly to outward shew. Formed like dolls or play-things, which are given to children to captivate by outside appearances, they are generally rendered incapable of exhibiting great talents, or of occupying an important station in life.

But it seems to have been reserved for the Quakers us a religious body, to insist upon that full practical treatment and estimation of women, which ought to take place wherever Christianity is professed. They have accordingly given to the females of their own society their proper weight in the scale of created beings. Believing them to have adequate capacities, and to be capable of great usefulness, they have admitted them to a share in the administration of almost all the offices which belong to their religious discipline, so that, independently of their private, they have a public character, like the men.

In the first volume, I had occasion to observe, when treating on the subject of the discipline, that representatives were chosen by the men out of their own body to the different meetings which were then named. Just so it is with the Quaker women. Representatives are appointed out of these by the other women on similar occasions. I stated also that, at certain times, the men assembled by themselves; that they discussed the business that came before them; that they replied to those who supported opposite opinions to their own; and that the young men were present during these discussions. So it is with the women. They sit in council by themselves. They argue and reply in like manner. The young females are also present. I stated also, that during these meetings of the men, one of them held the office of drawing up and recording the minutes of the proceedings or resolutions that had taken place. The women also appoint one of their own body to the same office. I stated again, that, in these meetings of the men, some were chosen as a committee to act in particular cases. So also are women chosen to act as a committee by their own meetings. I explained the nature of the office of overseer, and I observed that there were overseers among the men. There are also overseers among the women. I explained the nature of the office of elder, and I observed that there were elders among the men. The women have their elders likewise. The men were said to preach as in other societies. The women are permitted to preach also. In short, if the men consider themselves to be qualified for any office belonging their religious discipline, they believe their women to be equally capable of holding the same. No distinction is made as to the powers of usefulness between the men and the women of this society. There are few offices held by men, but there is a corresponding one for those of the other sex.

[Footnote 41: The principal exceptions are, that they are not correspondents, arbitrators, legislators, or on committees of appeal.]

The execution of these and other, public offices, by which the Quaker women have an important station allotted them in society, cannot but have an important influence on their minds. It gives them, in fact, a new cast of character. It imparts to them, in the first place, a considerable knowledge of human nature. It produces in them thought, and foresight, and judgment. It creates in them a care and concern for the distressed. It elevates their ideas. It raises in them a sense of their own dignity and importance as human beings, which sets them above every thing that is little and trifling, and above all idle parade and shew. Fond as they are of the animal creation, you do not see them lavishing their caresses on lap-dogs, to the contempt of the poor and miserable of their own species. You never see them driving from shop to shop to make up a morning's amusement, by examining and throwing out of order the various articles of tradesmen, giving them great trouble, and buying nothing in return. You never find them calling upon those whom they know to be absent from their homes, thus making their mimic visits, and leaving their useless cards. Nothing, in short, so ridiculous or degrading, is known among them. Their pursuits are rational, useful, and dignified. And they may be said in general to exhibit a model for the employment of time, worthy of the character they profess.

MISCELLANEOUS PARTICULARS RELATIVE TO THE QUAKERS

Quakers a happy people—Subordinate causes of this happiness—namely, their comfortable situation—their attachment to domestic life—their almost constant employment—this happiness not broken like that of others, by an interruption of the routine of constituted pleasures—or by anger and other passions or by particular enquiries and notions about religion.

If a person were to judge of the Quakers by the general gravity of their countenances, and were to take into consideration, at the same time, the circumstance, that they never partook of the amusements of the world, in which he placed a part of his own pleasures, he would be induced to conclude, that they had dull and gloomy minds, and that they could not be upon the whole a happy people. Such a conclusion, however, would be contrary to the fact. On my first acquaintance with them I was surprised, seeing the little variety of their pursuits, at the happiness which they appeared to enjoy, but as I came to a knowledge of the constitution and state of the society, the solution of the problem became easy.

It will not be difficult to develope the subordinate causes of this happiness. To shew the first of these, I shall view the society in the three classes of the rich, the middle, and the poor. Of the rich, I may observe, that they are not so affluent in general as the rich of other bodies. Of the middle, that they are upon the whole in better circumstances than others of the same class in life. Of the poor, that they are not so poor as others in a similar condition. Now the rich in the Quaker society have of course as many of the comforts of life in their power as they desire. The middle classes in this society have more of these than the middle classes of other denominations. The poor in the same society have also more of these, in consequence of the handsome provision which is made for them, than others in a similar situation with themselves. There is therefore upon the whole a greater distribution of the comforts of life, among all the ranks of this society, than is to be found in any other community, in proportion to their numbers. But this superior state, in point of comfortable circumstances, ought to be undoubtedly a source of superior happiness. For where the comforts of life are wanting, it is in vain to suppose men can be happy, unless their minds are more than usually comforted by their religion.

[Footnote 42: Religion, which includes positive virtues, and an absence from vices, joined to a peaceful conscience and a well grounded hope of a better life, is the first and greatest cause of happiness, and may belong to all.

But I confine myself, in this chapter, to such causes only as may be called subordinate, and in which the Quakers are more particularly concerned.]

Another source of their happiness may be found in their domestic situation. The Quakers, as I have observed before, in consequence of denying themselves the pleasures of the world, have been obliged to cherish those which are found in domestic life. In the fashionable world, men and their wives seldom follow their pleasures together. They resemble the little wooden figures of the man and the woman, which, by moving backwards and forwards in a small painted house, denote the changes of the weather. While one of these is within, the other is out of doors. But this is not the case with the Quakers. The husband and wife are not so easily separable. They visit generally together. They are remarked as affectionate. You never hear of intrigues among them. They are long in each others society at a time, and they are more at home than almost any other people. For neither the same pleasures, nor the same occupations, separate these as others. The husband is never seen at a play, nor at a tavern, nor at a dance. Neither the naval nor the military profession summons him abroad. He is seldom concerned in voyages as a mariner. Hence he must of necessity be much at home. Add to this, that the Quakers have generally families, with the power of providing for them. But these circumstances render their homes agreeable to them, and increase their domestic delights.

A third source of the happiness of the Quakers arises from the circumstance of their being almost constantly employed. Few are so miserable as those who have nothing to do, or who, unable to find employment, feel a dull vacuum in their time. And the converse of this proposition is equally true, that the time of those flies pleasantly away, who can employ it rationally. But there is rarely such a being among the Quakers as a lazy person, gaping about for amusement. Their trades or callings occupy the greater portion of their time. Their meetings of discipline, as has been already shewn, occupy their time again. The execution of the various offices to which they may be appointed, such as of overseers, or elders, or committee-men, or arbitrators in disputes, occupies more. Few Quakers, but particularly the more respectable, have many vacant hours. And here it may not be improper to remark, that the discipline of the society, organized as it is, is productive of a cheerful and friendly intercourse of the members, or of a sociable manner of spending their time, one with another. The monthly meetings usually bring two or three particular meetings together. The members of these, when they have dispatched their business, retire to the houses of their friends, where they take their refreshment, and indulge in the pleasures of conversation. The quarterly meetings again bring the monthly meetings of the county into one. Here again, when the business is over, they partake of a similar repast. Hence a renewal of conversation and of friendship. The yearly meeting again brings many, from the quarterly together. And here the Quakers from all parts of the kingdom have an opportunity of seeing and conversing with one another. I may add too, that many individuals in the interim, who travel, whether on business or on pleasure, or on religious errands, enlarge this friendly intercourse; for few Quakers pass through the towns where Quakers live, without calling upon these, so that there are many sources within the customs and constitution of the society, that are productive of cheerful hours.

[Footnote 43: It may be mentioned here, that the Quakers acknowledge their relations to a much farther degree of consanguinity, than other people. This relationship, where it can be distinctly traced, is commemorated by the appellation of cousin. This custom therefore is a cause of endearment when they meet, and of course of additional pleasure.]

But here it will probably be said, that these sources of happiness, which have been hitherto described, are common to many others. I grant they are to individuals, but not to communities at large. No society has probably so many of the comforts of life in its power, number for number, and rank for rank, as that of the Quakers. None probably so wholly domestic. None, where the members of it have such frequent intercourse with each other, or where they are so connected in the bonds of brotherly love, and none, as far as I know men, who have such constant employment for their time.

Having explained some of those, which may be considered as positive sources of happiness to the Quakers, I shall now shew what may be causes of unhappiness to others, and that the Quakers seldom partake of these. Such an exposition, however strange it may appear at the first sight, will be materially to the point. For though an exemption from the causes of the uneasiness of others can never be admitted as a proof of the existence of positive enjoyment among the Quakers, yet if the latter have solid sources of happiness of their own, and these are not in any material degree diminished by the causes of the uneasiness of the former, there will be left to them, because there will be no drawback, a certain portion of happiness with less alloy. And here it is obvious at the first sight, that the Quakers have not the same, nor so many wants as others, with respect to their pleasures, and that they do not admit the same things to be component parts of them. Hence they have not the same causes of uneasiness from the chance of interruption. Hence also their happiness is more in their own power. What individual can annihilate the comforts which arise from their own industry, or their domestic enjoyments, or their friendly intercourse with each other, or their employments, which arise from their discipline, and from their trade and callings? But how easily are many of the reputed enjoyments of the world to be broken? Some people place their happiness in a routine of constituted pleasures. In proportion as these have been frequently resorted to, they will have got into the habit as the necessary enjoyments of life. Take away then from persons in such habits the power of these their ordinary gratifications, and you will make them languid, and even wretched. There will be a wide chasm, which they will not know how to fill up; a dull vacuum of time, which will make their existence insipid; a disappointment, which will carry with it a lacerating sting. In some of the higher circles of life, accustomed to such rounds of pleasure, who does not know that the Sunday is lamented as the most cruel interrupter of their enjoyments?—No shopping in the morning—no theatre or route in the evening—Nothing but dull heavy church stares them in the face. But I will not carry this picture to the length to which I am capable. I shall only observe that, where persons adopt a routine of constituted pleasures, they are creating fictitious wants for themselves, and making their own happiness subject to interruption, and putting it into the power of others. The Quakers, however, by the total rejection of all the amusements included in the routine alluded to, know nothing of the drawbacks or disadvantages described.

The Quakers again are exempt from several of the causes of uneasiness, which attach to the world at large. Some go to the gaming-table, and ruin themselves and their families, and destroy the peace of their minds. But the Quakers are never found injuring their fortunes or their happiness by such disreputable means.

Others disturb the harmony of their lives by intemperate sallies of passion. It has been well observed, that, whatever may be the duration of a man's anger, so much time he loses of the enjoyment of his life. The Quakers, however, have but few miserable moments on this account. A due subjugation of the passions has been generally instilled into them from early youth. Provocation seldom produces in them any intemperate warmth, or takes away, in any material degree, from the apparent composure of their minds.

Others again, by indulging their anger, are often hurried into actions of which the consequences vex and torment them, and of which they often bitterly repent. But the Quakers endeavour to avoid quarrelling, and therefore they often steer clear of the party and family feuds of others. They avoid also, as much as possible, the law, so that they have seldom any of the lawsuits to harass and disturb them, which interrupt the tranquillity of others by the heavy expence, and by the lasting enmities they occasion.

The Quakers again are exempt from many of the other passions which contribute to the unhappiness of the world at large. Some men have an almost boundless ambition. They are desirous of worldly honours, or of eminent stations, or of a public name, and pursue these objects in their passage through life with an avidity which disturbs the repose of their minds. But the Quakers scarcely know any such feeling as that of ambition, and of course scarcely any of the torments that belong to it. They are less captivated by the splendour of honours than any other people, and they had rather live in the memory of a few valuable friends, than be handed down to posterity for those deeds, which generally constitute the basis of public character.

Others again, who cannot obtain these honourable distractions, envy those who possess them. They envy the very coronet upon the coach, as it passes by. But the Quakers can have no such feelings as these. They pass in their pilgrimage through life regardless of such distinctions, or they estimate them but as the baubles of the, day. It would be folly therefore to suppose, that they could be envious of that which they do not covet.

The Quakers again are exempt from some of the occasions of uneasiness which arise to others from considerations on the subject of religion. Some people, for example, pry into what are denominated mysteries. The more they look into these, the less they understand them, or rather, the more they are perplexed and confounded. Such an enquiry too, while it bewilders the understanding, generally affects the mind. But the Quakers avoid all such curious enquiries as these, and therefore they suffer no interruption of their enjoyment from this source. Others again, by the adoption of gloomy creeds, give rise frequently to melancholy, and thus lay in for themselves a store of fuel for the torment of their own minds. But the Quakers espouse no doctrines, which, while they conduct themselves uprightly, can interrupt the tranquillity of their lives. It is possible there may be here and mere an instance where their feelings may be unduly affected, in consequence of having carried the doctrine of the influence of the Spirit, as far as it relates to their own condition, beyond its proper bounds. But individuals, who may fell into errors of this nature, are, it is to be hoped, but few; because any melancholy, which may arise from these causes, must be the effect, not of genuine Quakerism, but of a degenerate superstition.

CHAP. II.

Good, which the Quakers have done as a society upon earth—by their general good example—by shewing that persecution for religion is ineffectual—by shewing the practicability of the subjugation of the will of man—the influence of Christianity on character—the inefficacy of capital punishments—the best object of punishment—the practicability of living, either in a private or a public capacity, in harmony and peace—the superiority of the policy of the Gospel over the policy of the world.

When we consider man as distinguished from other animals by the rational and spiritual faculties which he possesses, we cannot but conceive it to be a reproach to his nature, if he does not distinguish himself from these, or, if he does not leave some trace behind him, that he has existed rationally and profitably both to himself and others. But if this be expected of man, considered abstractedly as man, much more will it be expected of him, if he has had the advantages of knowing the doctrines of Christianity, and the sublime example of the great Author of that religion. And the same observation, I apprehend, will hold true with respect to societies of men. For if they have done no good during their existence, we cannot see how they can escape censure, or that it would not have been better that they had not existed at all. This consideration leads me to enquire, what good the Quakers have done since their institution, as a society, upon earth.

It was said of the Quakers in George Fox's time, after their character had been established, that, "if they did not stand, the nation would run into debauchery." By this I apprehend it was meant, that it was a desirable thing to have a people to look up to, who, residing in the 'midst of a vicious community, professed to be followers of that which was right, and to resist the current of bad example in their own times; or that such a people might be considered as a leaven, that might leaven the whole lump, but that, if this leaven were lost, the community might lose one of its visible incitements to virtue. Now in this way the Quakers have had a certain general usefulness in the world. They have kept more, I apprehend, to first principles, than any other people. They have afforded a moral example. This example ought to have been useful to others. To those who were well inclined, it should have been as a torch to have lighted up their virtue, and it should have been a perpetual monument for reproof to others, who were entering upon a career of vice.

The first particular good, after the general one now stated, which the Quakers have done, has been, that they have shewn to those who have been spectators of their conduct, that all persecution for matters of religion, as it is highly criminal in the eyes of the Supreme Being, so it is inadequate to the end proposed. This proposition, indeed, seems to be tolerably Well understood at the present day. At least they whose minds have been well informed, acknowledge it. The history of martyrdom, by which we learn how religion soars above all suffering, how the torments inflicted on the body are unable to reach the mind, how the moral Governor of the world reigns triumphant upon earth, how tyranny and oppression fall prostrate before virtue, losing their malignant aim, has been one, among other causes, of this knowledge. But as history is known but to few, and is not remembered by all, the Quakers are particularly useful by holding up the truth of the proposition to our daily sight, that is, by the example they continue to afford us of bearing their testimony in all cases where the civil magistrate is concerned on the one hand, and their consciences on the other.

A second good, which the Quakers have done, is by shewing, as a whole body, the power of Christianity in the subjugation of the will of men, and its influence on their character.

They are living proofs, in the first instance, that human nature is not the stubborn thing, which many have imagined it to be; that, however it may be depraved, it is still corrigible; and that this correction is universally practicable, for that there are as various dispositions in this society as in any other in proportion to its numbers. They shew, that Christianity can alter the temper, that it can level enmities, and that there is no just occasion for any to despair. And they are living proofs, in the second, as to what kind of character Christianity, where it is rightly received, will produce; They are living proofs, that it can produce sobriety, inoffensiveness, simplicity, charity, peace, and the domestic and other virtues. Now though every private Christian can shew in himself an example of these effects, yet the Quakers shew it, not by producing solitary instances, but as a body; the temper of the great mass of their members being apparently cast in the same mould, and their character, as a society, being acknowledged to be that of a moral people.

And here I cannot but stop for a moment to pay a just tribute to the Quaker system, as one of the best modes of the Christian Religion; for whether the doctrines which belong to it, or whether the discipline which it promotes, or whether both of them conjointly, produce the effects which have been just related, certain it is, that they are produced. But that system of religion is surely the most excellent, which produces, first, the greatest, and, secondly, the most universal effect upon those who profess it. For what is the use of any particular creed, or where is the advantage of any one creed above another, if it cannot give the great characteristic marks of a Christian, a subjugated mind and a moral character? What signifies the creed of any particular description of Christian professors, if it has no influence on the heart, or if we see professors among these giving way to their passions, or affording an inconsistent example to the world.

[Footnote 44: Many of the Quakers in America, influenced by custom, Adopted the practice of holding slaves. But on a due recurrence to their principles they gave freedom to these unconditionally, thus doing another public good in the world, and giving another example of the power of religion on the mind.]

The Quakers have given, again, in the reforms, which, in the first volume, I described them to have introduced into legislation, a beautiful and practical lesson of jurisprudence to the governors of all nations. They have shewn the inefficacy of capital punishments; that the best object in the punishment of offenders is their reformation; that this accords best with the genius and spirit of the Christian Religion; and that while such a system, when followed, restores the abandoned to usefulness in society, it diminishes the number of crimes.

[Footnote 45: See Vol. I, Sect. 4, p. 198.]

They have shewn again, by their own example, that it is not so difficult for men to live peaceably together, as has been usually believed; and they have exhibited the means by which they have effected this desirable end in life. And as they have proved, that this is practicable in private, so they have proved, as has appeared in this volume, that it is practicable in public life, or, which is the same thing, they have shewn, that in the intercourse which exists between nations, there is no necessity for wars.

They have shewn and established again by the two latter instances, both of which relate to government, a proposition which seems scarcely to be believed, if we judge by the practice of statesmen, but the truth of which ought for ever to be insisted upon, that the policy of the Gospel is superior to the policy of the world.

This is a portion of the good which the Quakers have done since their appearance as a society in the world. What other good they have done it is not necessary to specify. And as to what they would do, if they were permitted to become universal legislators, it may be a pleasing subject for contemplation, but it does not fall within the limits of the present chapter.

CHAP. III.

I have often heard it suggested as matter for conversation, whether the Quakers were increasing or decreasing in their number, and the result has always been an opinion, that they were a declining body.

When we consider the simplicity and even philosophy of the Quaker religion, the preservation it affords against the follies and difficulties of life, and the happiness to which it ultimately leads, we shall wonder that the progress of the society, in point of number, has not been greater than we find it. And when we consider, on the other hand, how difficult it is to be a Quaker, how much it is against the temper and disposition of man to be singular, or to resist the tide of custom and fashion, and to undergo an ordeal of suffering on these accounts, we shall wonder that it has not been long ago extinct.

That many are disowned by the society, in consequence of which its numbers are diminished, is true. That others come into it from other quarters, by which an increase is given to it, independently of its own natural population, is true also. But whether the new members exceed the disowned, or the disowned the new, is the question to be resolved. Now no people have had better opportunities of ascertaining this point, than the Quakers themselves. By means of their monthly meetings they might with ease have instituted a census on a given day. They might have renewed such a census. They might have compared the returns in every case. But as no such census has ever been made, the Quakers themselves, though they have their ideas, cannot speak with particular accuracy, on this subject.

The general opinion, however, is, and the Quakers, I apprehend, will not deny but lament it, that those who go out of the society are upon the whole more numerous than those who come into it by convincement, and therefore that there is, upon the whole, a decrease among them.

Of the truth of this opinion, some have adduced as a proof, that the quarterly meetings have been reduced to three fourths of their original number. But this is not to be considered as a certain criterion of the fact. For it is by no means uncommon to find, if the Quakers decrease in one county, that they increase in another. It has also been adduced, that many particular meetings have been broken up, or that meeting-houses in the country are standing deserted, or without Quakers to worship in them. But neither can this be considered as any infallible proof of the point. For it frequently happens, that if the Quakers become less numerous in any particular village, they become more so in some of the towns of the same county. Thus no true judgment can be formed upon these principles. The Quaker population, in this respect, on account of its movements, resembles the sea, which, while it loses on one part of its shores or boundaries, gains upon another.

There are, however, considerations, which may be more decisive of the fact.

In the time of George Fox the number of those converted to his principles was immense. This number, if we consult all the facts that might be adduced on the occasion, continued to be large in after times. Now it must be observed, that the Quakers are a sober and temperate people, that they generally marry at a proper age, and that they have large families. It is therefore impossible, if the descendants of the early Quakers had continued in the society, that their number should not have been much larger than we find it at the present day, and, if so, there must have been a secession or an expulsion, amounting, notwithstanding all influx by conversion, to a decrease.

[Footnote 46: Although the remark may be just, that in the time of George Fox "a great number were converted to his principles," yet a small portion of those were actually received into membership, and the same remark may correctly be made even in the present day: as it is believed that immense numbers are convinced of the truth as held by the Quakers, but owing to their "not being willing to undergo an ordeal of suffering on account of their principles," a small portion of those apply to be admitted into the society. AMERICAN EDITOR.]

It is obvious again that the Quakers, in consequence of their industry and their frugal habits, must almost unavoidably grow rich. Now if the descendants of the early Quakers had remained in the society, we should have seen more overgrown fortunes in it, than among others in proportion to their numbers. But this is contrary to the fact. The very richest, as the world now goes, would not be considered to be particularly rich; and it is a truth that those who are affluent among them have generally been the founders, by means of their industry and integrity, of their own fortunes.

It is, again, a matter of observation among the Quakers, now grown into a truth, that if men grow rich in the society, their grand-children generally leave it. But surely this amounts to a confession, that in a particular part of the society there are the seeds of a regular and successive decrease.

That the Quakers then upon the whole are a declining body, there can be no doubt. While I state it, I lament it. I lament that there should be any diminution of number among those who have done so much good in the world, and who have so justly obtained the reputation of a moral people. This consideration will lead me to enquire into the causes of this decline. It will impel me also to enquire into the means of remedy. How far I may be successful in the latter attempt, I am unable to say. But it will always be a pleasing consideration to me, to have tried to prevent the decrease of a virtuous people.

[Footnote 47: Against this decrease we cannot set off any great increase by admission into membership. The dress, the language, the fear of being singular, the discipline with its various restraints, the unwillingness of men to suffer where suffering can be avoided, these and other circumstances are great impediments in the way of an entrance into this society; and to this I may add, that applications for admission into it are not always complied with.]

With respect then to the causes of this decline, to which I shall confine myself in this chapter, they will be found in the causes of disownment. Now of these, some may be called original and immediate, and others original and remote.

Of original and immediate, the first is what the Quakers call mixed marriage. It has been before stated, that those who marry out of the society are disowned, and the reasons for such disownments have been given.

A second will be found in tithes. They who pay these are ultimately disowned. And they are disowned as well for the payment of lay-tithes, as of those which are ecclesiastical.

Of the original and remote, a very prolific cause is the pursuit of trade, connected as it is with the peculiar habits of the society, and a residence in the towns.

[Footnote 48: Owing perhaps to the causes alleged by the author, the society may have decreased in England, yet it is certain that in this country the number of Quakers has very considerably increased. AMERICAN EDITOR.]

To shew this I must observe, first, that the poor, comparatively speaking, are seldom disowned, for they know that they shall never be so well provided for in any other society. I must observe again, that the members of the middle classes are also, comparatively speaking, but seldom disowned. These must live by trade, but if so, they cannot be better off than as Quakers. The direct conclusion then, from these observations, will be, that the greater number of those who are disowned, will be found among the rich, or among such as are growing rich. Hence it appears, that, as far as this original and remote cause is concerned, my enquiry must be, how it happens, that members of this particular class should be excluded from membership more than those of any other.

[Footnote 49: I by no means intend to say, that the poor do not remain in the society from an attachment to its principles, but that this may be a political motive also.]

In answer to this enquiry I must say, as I have observed before, that Quakers in trade, having as good abilities, and as much diligence and integrity as others, will succeed as well as others in it, but that, having less sources of outgoings, their savings will be generally greater. Hence they will have before their eyes the sight of a greater accumulation of wealth. But in proportion as such accumulation of substance is beheld, the love of it increases. Now while this love increases, or while their hearts are unduly fixed on the mammon of the world, they allow many little inconsistencies in their children to escape their reproof. But, besides this, as the religion and the love of the mammon of the world are at variance, they have a less spiritual discernment than before. Hence they do not see the same irregularities in the same light. From this omission to check these irregularities on the one hand, and from this decay of their spiritual vision on the other, their children have greater liberties allowed them than others in the same society. But as these experience this indulgence, or as these admit the customs and fashions of the world, they grow more fond of them. Now, as they live in towns, the spark that is excited is soon fanned into a flame. Fashions and fashionable things, which they cannot but see daily before their eyes, begin to get the dominion. When they are visited by wholesome advisers, they dislike the interference. They know they shall be rich. They begin to think the discipline of the society a cruel restraint. They begin to dislike the society itself, and, committing irregularities, they are sometimes in consequence disowned. But, if they should escape disownment themselves, they entail it generally upon their children. These are brought up in a still looser manner than themselves. The same process goes on with these as with their parents, but in a still higher degree, till a conduct utterly inconsistent with the principles of the society occasions them to be separated from it. Thus in the same manner, as war, according to the old saying, begets poverty, and poverty peace, so the pursuit of trade, with the peculiar habits of the society, leads to riches, riches to fashion and licentiousness, and fashion and licentiousness to disownment, so that many Quakers educate their children as if there were to be no Quakers in the second generation from themselves. And thus, though, strictly speaking, irregularities are the immediate occasion of these disownments, they are ultimately to be attributed to the original and remote cause as now described.

[Footnote 50: I hope I shall not be understood as involving the rich in a promiscuous censure. I know as amiable examples among these and among their children, as among others of the society. But we must naturally expect more deviations among the rich, number for number, than among others.]

That this is by no means an unreasonable account, I shall shew in some measure by an appeal to facts. The American Quakers sprang from the English. The English, though drained in consequence, were still considerable, when compared with the former. But it is remarkable, that the American Quakers exceed the English by at least five times their number at the present day. Now it must undoubtedly be confessed, that the Americans have advantages, as far as this fact is concerned, which the English have not. They have no tithes as a cause of disownment. Their families also, I believe, increase more rapidly. Many persons also, as will be the case in a country that is not fully settled, live in the neighbourhoods of the Quakers, but at a distance from those of other religious denominations, and therefore, wishing to worship somewhere, seek membership with them. But I apprehend that a great cause of this disparity of number lies in this difference of the situation of the two, that whereas the great Quaker population in England is in the towns with but a remnant in the country, the great Quaker population in America is in the country with but a remnant in the towns. And that the Americans themselves believe, that the place of the residence of their members is connected in some measure with the increase and decrease of their society, it is fair to presume, from this circumstance, that, in several of the quarterly meetings in America, advice has been given to parents to bring up their children in the country, and, as little as possible, in the towns.

[Footnote 51: The number of the Quakers is undoubtedly great in one or two of the cities in America, but the whole town-population is not great, when compared with the whole country-population there.]

Another of the original and remote causes is education. This, as it becomes promotive of the diminution of the society, is of two kinds. The first may be called alien. The second is such as is afforded in the society itself.

Some parents, growing rich, and wishing to give their children a better education, than they can get in their own schools, send them to others to be instructed. Now the result has not been desirable, where it has been designed, that such children should be continued Quakers. For how is a poor solitary Quaker boy to retain the peculiarities belonging to his religious profession, in the face of the whole school? Will not his opinions and manners be drowned as it were in the torrent of the opinions and manners of the rest? How can he get out of this whirlpool pure? How, on his return, will he harmonize with his own society? Will not either he, or his descendants, leave it? Such an education may make him undoubtedly both a good and an enlightened man, and so far one of the most desirable objects in life will have been accomplished, but it certainly tends to destroy the peculiar institution of Quakerism.

The education, which is afforded in the society itself, is divisible again into two kinds, into that which is moral or religious, and into that which is literary or philosophical.

It must undoubtedly be confessed, in looking into that which is moral or religious, that sufficient care is not always taken with regard to youth. We sometimes see fathers and sons, and mothers and daughters, so different in their appearance and deportment, that we should scarcely have imagined them to be of the same family. I am not now speaking of those parents, who may live in the towns, and who may be more than ordinarily devoted to the mammon of the world, but of some who, living both in town and country, give an example of a liberal and amiable spirit, and of a blameless conduct to the world. That the former should neglect and lose sight of their offspring, when their moral vision is clouded by an undue eagerness after money, is not to be wondered at, but that the latter should do it, is surprising. It is certainly true that some of these are too indulgent in their families, contrary to the plan and manner of their own education, or that they do not endeavour to nip all rising inconsistencies in the bud. The consequence is, that their children get beyond control in time, when they lament in vain their departure from the simplicity of the society. Hence the real cause of their disownment, which occasionally follows, is not in the children running out of bounds, but in the parents running out of bounds in the manners of their children. And here I may add, that some parents, dwelling too much on the disuse of forms in religion, because such disuse is inculcated by their own doctrines, run into the opposite extreme, and bring up their children in too much ignorance of the general plan of Christianity, as it is laid down in the letter of the scriptures.

With respect to education, as for it is literary or philosophical, it is frequently sufficient for those upon whom it is bestowed. But it does not appear to me to be carried to its proper extent, in the case of the children of the rich, when I consider how friendly it might be made towards the promotion of virtue. Some, we know, growing wealthy, have had children when they were poorer, and, when in this poorer state, they have given them an education which has been suitable to it, not calculating upon their future rise in life. But their children, having had such a limited education, have not had that which has been proper for their subsequent station in life. Others again, who have been born in better circumstances, have, on account of an undue depreciation of human knowledge, educated their children as improperly for their station as the former. The children then, in both these cases, have not had an education sufficient, with the prospect of riches before them, to keep them out of the way of harm. They have not had, in addition to any religious instruction, that taste given them for sublime pursuits, which should make them despise those which were frivolous. Thus many of the corruptive opinions, fashions, and amusements of the world have charmed them. Giving way to these, they have been overcome. When overcome, they have run into excesses, and for these excesses they have been disowned. But surely, with a better education, they would have thought all such corruptive opinions, fashions, and amusements, as below their notice, and unworthy of their countenance and support.

CHAP. IV.

Supposed remedies for the diminution of some of these causes—Regulations in the case of mixed marriages—Measures to be adopted in the pursuit of trade—Education, as it is moral or religious, to be more strictly enforced in some families—as it is literary or philosophical, to be carried to a greater extent among the children of the rich—Object of this latter education—Nature of it as consisting both knowledge and prohibitions—How it would operate against the fascinating allurements of the world, or to the end proposal.

I Purpose now to suggest, as briefly as I can, such opinions, as, if adopted, might possibly operate as remedies to some of the evils which have been described. In doing this I am aware of the difficulties that await me. I am sensible that I ought not to be too sanguine as to the result of all my observations upon this subject and yet, I cannot but think, that I may be successful in some of them. Arduous, however, as the task, and dubious as my success may be, I am encouraged, on the prospect of being but partially useful, to undertake it.

On the first of the original and immediate causes which have been mentioned, I mean mixed marriages, I shall have but little to say. I do not see how it is possible, while the society means to keep up a due subordination among its members, not to disown such as may marry out of it. In mixed families, such as these marriages produce, it is in vain to expect that the discipline can be carried on, as has been shewn in the second volume. And, without this discipline, the society would hardly keep up, in the extensive manner it does, the character of a moral people. I think, however, that some good might be done by regulations to be universally observed. Thus they, who are deputed to inform the disowned of their exclusion from membership, should be of the most amiable temper and conciliatory manners. Every unqualified person should be excluded from these missions. Permission should be solicited for both the married persons to be present on such occasions. It is difficult to estimate the good effect which the deputed, if of sweet and tender dispositions, or the bad effects which the deputed, if of cold and austere manners, might have upon those they visited, or what bias it might give the one in particular, who had never been in membership, for or against the society. Permission also might be solicited, even when the mission was over for future friendly opportunities or visits, which would shew in the society itself a tender regard and solicitude for the welfare of its former members. It is not at all improbable, from the impression which such apparent regard and solicitude might occasion, that the children of the visited, though not members, might be brought up in the rules of membership. And finally it appears to me to be desirable, that the disowned, if they should give proof by their own lives and the education of their children, of their attachment to the principles of the society, and should solicit restoration to membership, should be admitted into it again without any acknowledgment of past errors, and wholly as new and convinced members.

With respect to the second of the immediate and original causes, which is to be found in tithes, I may observe that it is, as for as I can collect, but a small and an inferior one, few being disowned on this account, and still fewer now than formerly. It would be desirable, however, few as these instances may be, to prevent them. But I fear that no remedy can be pointed out, in which the Quakers would acquiesce, except it could be shewn, that a distinction might be made between the payment of ecclesiastical and lay-tithes, which would not interfere with the great tenets of the society on this subject.

A third cause of disownment, but this belongs to the original and remote, was shewn to be the pursuit of trade, connected as it is with the peculiar habits of the society and a residence in the towns. I may propose as remedies for this, first, that parents should be careful to exhibit a good example to their children. Secondly, as I have before observed, that they should prescribe to themselves moderation in the acquisition of wealth, either by relinquishing trade at a given time, or by dealing out the profits of it more liberally than common in the way of benevolence, so that their children, in each case, may never have the misfortune of the prospect of a large moneyed independence before their eyes. Or lastly, that they should give them a better education than they do at present, on which subject, according to the prescribed order of things, I am now to speak.

A fourth cause then, but this belongs also to the original and remote, was shewn to exist in education. And education, as it was promotive of the diminution of the society, was of two kinds.

With respect to that part of it which is alien, the remedy is easy. There has been great difficulty in procuring proper schoolmasters, I mean such as have been Quakers. Two reasons may be given for this. The first is, that the society having been backward in affording due encouragement to learning, few of any great literary acquisitions have been brought up in it. The second is, that persons have found, that they could make much less of their time in such a line of employment than in the way of trade. But surely the Quakers, as a body in comfortable and independent circumstances, might easily remedy the evil. Does not a man, who devotes his time to the instruction of youth, deserve to be made as comfortable as the man who sells silver utensils, or bracelets, or ear-rings, or other articles of trade? Is there any comparison between the moral usefulness of these? Is there any profession more useful than that which forms the youthful mind? or rather, is it not the most important profession in the state?

[Footnote 52: It is but justice to the Quakers to observe, that they are taking more pains than formerly in the promotion of this object. I am told that there are more private seminaries now kept by Quakers for the education of the youth of their own society, than even before the institution of Ackworth school.]

With respect to the education which is acquired in the society itself, the remedy is not difficult. This education was shewn to be of two kinds.

On that part of it, which is moral or religious, I may observe, that the remedy is in the parents themselves. The first thing to be recommended is an universal vigilance over the disposition and manners of children, so that no censurable appearance, whether in temper or in conduct, may be allowed to pass without suitable notice or reproof, or that the bud, which promises to be corruptive of morals, should no sooner make its appearance, than it should be cut off. In cases of so much importance, as where the happiness both of parents and children is concerned, the former should be peculiarly circumspect. They should not talk about things, but insist upon them, on all proper occasions. They should not point out, but redress. They should not lop off the branches, but lay the axe to the root. And surely youth is the best season for such wholesome interference. It is, in the first place, the season in which a remedy is practicable; for we are assured, "if we train up a child in the way he should go, that, when he is old, he will not depart from it." It is, secondly, the season in which it is most practicable; for can we hope to bend the tree so easily to our form, as the sapling from whence it came? and, thirdly, it is the season in which it is practicable only, for will not a small irregularity grow, if uncontrolled, to a greater? Will not one irregularity also, if not properly checked, give birth to others? And may not these be so incorporated into the inner man in a course of time, that it may be as difficult for parents to eradicate them, as for the Ethiopian to change his colour, or the leopard his spots? But surely the Quakers ought to know the impropriety of undue indulgences in their families, as well as any other people? Is not the early subjugation of the will a doctrine more particularly adopted by them as a society? Without such a subjugation do they not conceive the mind to be in an unfit state to receive the admonitions of the pure principle, and of course to make a true proficiency in religion? Do they not consider themselves also as a highly professing people, and do they not know that the world expects more from them than from others? But how can their children ever perpetuate this extraordinary character after them, or shew that their parents possessed it, unless they are brought up in a peculiarly guarded manner? In addition to these observations it may be recommended, that parents should be careful to give their children what may be called a literal instruction in Christianity, in contradistinction to pure theism, or to those doctrines which they conceive may come from the teachings of the Holy Spirit, so that they may have a more intimate knowledge of all their principles, as a Christian body.

With respect to that part of education which may consist of knowledge as it is literary or philosophical, I conceive it might be attended with advantage to carry it to a greater extent than has hitherto been practised in the society, but particularly the latter. Nothing is so delightful to youth as experimental philosophy, by which they see the causes of things unfolded to their view. No science takes their attention more, or inclines them, in the farther pursuit of it, to be satisfied with home. And yet I doubt whether this branch of learning be not almost wholly neglected in the Quaker schools. The education which is received in the society, as it consists of the two kinds of knowledge described, is not, in my apprehension, carried far enough, so as to suit the peculiar situation of the children of the rich. These are they, who are most in danger. These are they, who, having the prospect of wealth before them, have the prospect of being able to procure destructive pleasures. These are they, who, having the prospect of independence, do not fear the opinion of the world or the loss of reputation in it, like those, who have their livelihood to obtain by their own industry. Now it should be the particular object of the education of these, as indeed it should be of all rich persons, so to instruct them, that, while they are obliged to live in the world, they may be enabled to live out of it, or deny it; so that, when seated amidst its corrupt opinions, amusements, and fashions, they should estimate them as below their notice, and as utterly unworthy of their countenance and support.

I should be sorry if, in holding up this species of education to a farther encouragement, as a preservative of the morals of the children of rich parents amidst the various temptations of life, I were to be thought to endeavour to take away in any degree the necessity of the influence of the Holy Spirit on the mind of man, or to deny that this Spirit ought not to be resorted to as the first and best guide, both by rich and poor, during their pilgrimage upon earth. For who can teach us best to deny the world? Who can teach us best to estimate its pursuits? Who can instruct us best to resist its temptations? To the Divine Being then we are first to look up, as to him who can be the best author of all our good, and the surest averter of all our evils, who can apply the best remedy to the imperfections of our nature, and who, while he leads us in safety, can lead us into the way of truth. But when we consider how many are inattentive, on account of the cares, and pleasures, and fashions, and prejudices, and customs of the world, to the secret notices of his grace, I cannot help considering that we may be allowed to have secondary and subordinate helps to our virtue. As the discipline of the Quaker society may produce and preserve a certain purity of life, so may a literary and philosophical education operate to the same end. Such an education is in its general tendency a friend to the promotion of virtue and to the discouragement of vice. It sets us often unquestionably above many of the corruptive opinions and customs in the midst of which we live. It leads us also frequently to the contemplation of the Divine Being in all the variety of his works. It gives us amiable, awful, and sublime conceptions of him. As far, therefore, as it is capable of doing this, it is a useful, though it be only a subordinate source of our purity, and we may therefore adopt it innocently. But we are never to forget, at the same time, that, though it may help us occasionally to resist corrupt temptations, and to encourage desirable propensities, yet it cannot do every thing for us that is necessary, and that we are never to overlook, on this account, the necessity of the influence of the Holy Spirit.

To shew in what the education, which under these limitations I am going to propose, may consist, I shall revive the controversy between the philosophical moralists and the Quakers, as described in the eighth chapter of the first volume. The philosophical moralists contended, that knowledge was to be preferred, as being more to be relied upon than prohibitions: that prohibitions were often causes of greater evils than they were intended to prevent; that they themselves were friends to occasional indulgencies; that they saw nothing necessarily or inherently mischievous in the amusements of the world; that it was not wise to anticipate danger by looking to distant prospects, where the things were innocent in themselves; that ignorance of vice was no guardian of morals; that causes, and not sub-causes, were to be contended against; and that there was no certain security but in knowledge and in a love of virtue. To this the Quakers replied, that prohibitions were sanctioned by divine authority; that as far as they related to the corrupt amusements of the world, they were implied in the spirit of Christianity; that the knowledge, which should be promotive of virtue, could not be inculcated without them; that knowledge again, if it were to be acquired by the permission of occasional indulgences, or by being allowed to pass through scenes which might be dangerous to virtue, would be more ruinous than ignorance by a prohibition of vice; that ignorance of vice was an essential in Christian morals; and that prohibitions therefore were indispensably necessary, and better to be relied upon, than any corrupt knowledge, which might arise from an acquaintance with the customs of the world.

This then was the state of the controversy, as described in the first volume. And in this state it was left. But, to explain the education which I have in view, I shall now bring it to a conclusion.

I must observe then, that the philosophical moralists had the advantage of the Quakers in this controversy, inasmuch as they supposed that knowledge was a better safeguard to morals than a mere ignorance of vice; but they failed in this, that they permitted this knowledge to be acquired by passing through scenes which might not be friendly to virtue. Now this latter permission is inadmissible in a Christian education; for no Christian youth ought to be permitted to see or to hear that which ought not to be uttered or exhibited by a Christian. The Quakers, on the other hand, had the advantage of the philosophical moralists, inasmuch as they considered ignorance to be better than corrupted knowledge; but they failed in this, that they seemed to rely upon ignorance of vice as a safeguard against it, without a proper portion of knowledge. The education then, to which I allude, ought to embrace the most valuable positions of both. It should consist of knowledge, and it should consist of wise prohibitions also. Knowledge and prohibitions are inseparable. While the mind is gaining knowledge, it should be kept innocent. And while it is kept innocent, it should be gaining knowledge. Youth should have that kind of knowledge instilled into them, by which they should discern the value of the prohibitions which are enjoined them. They should have such and so much knowledge, that if they were accidentally placed in the way of the things prohibited, they should be able to look them in the face, and pass through them without injury. This is that education, which, without superseding the necessity of the influence of the Holy Spirit, has a tendency to enable persons, while they live in the world, to live out of it or deny it.

But lest I should not be clearly understood upon this subject, I will exemplify how such an education would act or operate to the end proposed.

And, first of all, knowledge may be acquired by reading. Now there are two kinds of reading, the one useful, the other dangerous. By the premises, I am to adopt the first, and to prohibit the last. If then I accustom my child to the best and purest models of ancient and modern literature, I give him a certain taste for composition. If I accustom him to the purest and most amiable sentiments, as contained in these, I give him a love of virtue. If I heighten these sentiments by beautiful selections from the more pure and amiable sentiments of Christianity, I increase that love. If I give him in my own conduct an example, he sees me practise that which I recommend. I give him then a taste for the purest reading, and the choicest compositions, and I offer to his notice, at the same time, a certain system of morality, which he cannot but gradually adopt as his own. Now I would ask, what influence could a novel have upon a mind formed in this manner, if thrown accidentally in his way. If its composition were but moderate, as is the case with most of them, it would not suit the taste of my child. If its sentiments were impure, it would disgust him. These would be so contrary to the taste and to the feelings he had acquired, that the poison in such a book, like a ball, fired at a globular surface, would slide off without detriment to the morals of my child.

Knowledge again may be acquired in the course of amusements, and of such as may be resorted to within doors. Now of these again there are two kinds, the innocent and the corruptive. By the premises I am to be concerned with the first only. If then I accustom my child to mathematical and philosophical pursuits, if I incite him to experiments in these, if I assist him in measuring the motions of the heavenly bodies, and in discovering the wisdom and power of Omnipotence as displayed in these, if I occasion him to be interested in, the contemplation of such subjects, what have I done for my child? Have I not called out his intellectual faculties? Have I not laid in him the foundation of a serious and a thoughtful mind? Have I not accustomed him to solid things, in opposition to those that are light, and to sublime things, in opposition to those that are frivolous? Have I not inculcated in him a love for science? But take my child, after he has been accustomed to such thoughts and such subjects, to the theatre. Let the pantomime display its various attracting scenes to his view. And will he not think his entertainment low and superficial, in comparison of that which he left at home.

Knowledge again may be acquired by amusements which are out of doors. These again may be innocent or exceptionable. As before, I have nothing to do but with the former. If then I accustom my child to range the fields, as an employment promotive of his health, and connect this healthy exercise with the entertainment of botanical pursuits, do I not, in examining with him the shape, the colour, and the mechanism of plants and flowers, confirm in him his former love of the works of nature? Do I not confirm his former notion of the wisdom and power of omnipotence? Do I not teach him by these, and the other pursuits which have been mentioned, that all recreations should be innocent, and that time should be wisely employed? But hark! another amusement, and one of those which are followed out of doors, is at hand. The hounds are in view, and fast approaching. My son is accidentally solicited to join them. He would ask my permission, but I am absent. At length he goes. He follows them in wild tumult and uproar for an hour. He sees some galloping over hedges and ditches like madmen, and hazarding their persons in a presumptuous manner. He sees others ride over the cultivated fields of their neighbours, and injure the rising corn. He finds that all this noise and tumult, all this danger and injury, are occasioned by the pursuit of a little hare, whose pain is in proportion to the joy of those who follow it. Now can this diversion, educated as my child has been, fascinate him? Will he not question its innocence? And will he not question its consistency as a natural pursuit, or as an employment for his time?

It is thus then that knowledge will be found to operate as an artificial and innocent preservative against the destructive pleasures of the world. But prohibitions without knowledge will be but of little avail, where there is a prospect of riches, and the power of gratifying any improper appetites as they may arise. But by knowledge we shall be able to discover the beauty of things, so that their opposites, or the things prohibited, will cease to charm us. By knowledge we shall be able to discern the ugliness of the things prohibited, so that we shall be enabled to loathe them, if they should come into our way. And thus an education, conducted upon the principles of knowledge, may operate to the end proposed.

CHAP. V.

Education continued, as consisting of knowledge and prohibitions—Good, which the Quakers have done by prohibitions, without any considerable knowledge—Greater good, which they would do with it—Knowledge then a great desideratum in the Quaker education—Favourable state of the society for the communication of it with purity, or without detriment to morals—In what this knowledge should consist—General advantages of it—Peculiar advantages, which it would bring to the society.

When we consider that men have all the same moral nature, we wonder, at the first sight, at the great difference of conduct which they exhibit upon earth. But when we consider the power of education upon the mind, we seem to lose our surprize. If men in all countries were educated alike, we should find a greater resemblance in their character. It is, in short, education, which makes the man. And as education appears to me to be of so much importance in life, I shall make it the subject of this and the succeeding chapter.

All education should have two objects in view, the opening of the understanding and the improvement of the heart. Of the two, the latter is most important. There cannot be a question, whether the person of the most desirable character be the virtuous or the learned man. Without virtue knowledge loses half its value. Wisdom, without virtue, may be said to be merely political; and such wisdom, whenever it belongs to a man, is little better than the cunning or craftiness of a fox. A man of a cultivated mind, without an unshaken love of virtue, is but a dwarf of a man. His food has done him no good, as it has not contributed to his growth. And it would have been better, for the honour of literature, if he had never been educated at all. The talents of man, indeed, considering him as a moral being, ought always to be subservient to religion. "All philosophy, says the learned Cudworth, to a wise man, to a truly sanctified mind, as he in Plutarch speaketh, is but matter for divinity to work upon. Religion is the queen of all those inward endowments of the soul: and all pure natural knowledge, all virgin and undeflowered arts and sciences, are her handmaids, that rise up and call her blessed."

Now if the opening of the understanding, and the improvement of the heart, be the great objects to be attained, it will follow, that both knowledge and wise prohibitions should always be component parts of the education of youth. The latter the Quakers have adopted ever since the institution of their society. The former they have been generally backward to promote, at least to any considerable extent. That they have done good, however, by their prohibitions, though unaccompanied by any considerable knowledge, it would be disingenuous not to acknowledge. But this goad has been chiefly confined to the children of those who have occupied middle stations in the society. Such children have undoubtedly arrived at the true wisdom of life at an early age, as I described in the first volume, and have done honour to the religion they professed. But prohibitions, without knowledge, have not been found to answer so well among the children of those who have had the prospect of a large moneyed independence before them, and who have not been afraid either of the bad opinion of their own society, or of the bad opinion of the world. It has been shewn, however, that knowledge with prohibitions would, in all probability, be useful to these; that it would have a tendency to enable them, in the perilous situation in which they are placed, to stand against the corrupt opinions and fashions, and while they were living in the world, to live out of it, or to deny it.

Peculiarly situated as the Quakers are, they have opportunities, beyond any other people, of ingrafting knowledge into their system of education without danger, or, in other words, of giving knowledge to their children with the purity which Christianity would prescribe. The great misfortune in the world is, that a learned education is frequently thought more of than a virtuous one; that youth, while they are obtaining knowledge, are not properly watched and checked; and that they are suffered to roam at large in the pursuit of science, and to cultivate or not, at their own option, the science, if I may so call it, of religion. Hence it will happen, that, where we see learned men, we shall not always see these of the most exemplary character. But the Quakers have long ago adopted a system of prohibitions, as so many barriers against vice, or preservatives of virtue. Their constitution forbids all indulgences that appear unfriendly to morals. The Quakers therefore, while they retain the prohibitions which belong to their constitution, may give encouragement to knowledge, without a fear that it will be converted to the purposes of vice.

The Quakers, again, have opportunities or advantages, which others have not, in another point of view. In the great public seminary at Ackworth, which belongs to them, and which is principally for those who are of the poor and middle classes, every thing is under the inspection and guidance of committees, which can watch and enforce an observance of any rules that may be prescribed. Why then, if public seminaries were instituted for the reception of the children of the rich, or if the rich were to give encouragement to large private seminaries for the same purposes, should they not be placed under the visiting discipline of the society? Why should they not be placed under the care of committees also? Why should not these committees see that the two great objects of the education proposed were going on at the same time, or that, while knowledge was obtaining, discipline had not been relaxed. Why should not such seminaries produce future Penns, and Barclays, and others, who, while they were men capable of deep literary researches, should be exemplary for their virtue?

As knowledge then ought to form a part of the proposed education, on a much larger scale than has been hitherto encouraged, I shall say a few words as to the component parts of it, and as to the general advantages of these, and I shall afterwards speak to the advantages which the society in particular would derive from such a change.

In the education I propose, I do not mean, in the slightest manner, to break in upon the moral system of the Quakers, as described in the first volume. I do not propose to them the polite arts. I do not recommend them to make children musicians, or that they should learn, under the dancing-master, to step gracefully. I advise only such knowledge as will be strictly innocent and useful.

In the first place, I recommend a better classical education. Classical knowledge gives the foundation both of particular and universal grammar. While it gives the acquisition of the dead languages, it is the root, and therefore facilitates the acquisition of many of the living. As most of the technical terms in the professions and sciences are borrowed from these languages, it renders them easily understood. The study of the structure and combination of words and sentences calls forth the reflecting powers of youth, and expands their genius. It leads to penetration and judgement. It induces habits of diligence and patience. By means of this knowledge we have access to the sacred writings in the languages in which they were written, and we are therefore not liable to be imposed upon, for the sense of them, by others. We become acquainted also, by means of it, with the sentiments and knowledge of the ancients. We see their thoughts and expressions. We acquire a literary taste.

A knowledge of ancient history is necessarily conpected with the former. To this, however, should be added that of the modern. History, while it entertains us, instructs us morally. We cannot see the rise and fall of empires, or the causes of their formation and dissolution, or read the histories of good and bad men, without impressions of moral importance to ourselves.

A philosophical education is peculiarly important. By this I mean, a general knowledge of the mathematics, of mechanics, optics, hydrostatics, astronomy, chemistry, botany, and the like. The teaching of these should be accompanied by experiments. Experimental philosophy, as I observed before, is peculiarly interesting to youth. Such knowledge teaches us the causes of things. Mysteries, hitherto hidden both in the garden and in the field, and in the heaven and in the air, lie unfolded to our view. Every walk we take, while the surface of the earth remains as it is, and the canopy of the firmament is spread over us, gives its the opportunity, in all the innumerable objects presented to our view, of almost endless investigation and delight. And the deeper we go into the hidden things of nature, and the more we unfold them, have we not a better belief of the existence of the Creator, and grander notions of the symmetry, order, beauty, and wisdom of his works? Such knowledge leads also, as it has always done, to discoveries, by which we may make ourselves useful to mankind. And, besides the utility, of which it may make us capable, can discoveries of the principles of nature lessen oar love and admiration of the first great Cause?

To philosophical knowledge should be added general reading. Such reading should be of the purest kind. Of knowledge, acquired in this manner, it maybe said, that it opens new sources of right views and sentiments, and this even independently of Christianity, from which our most valuable information is derived. Thus at a time, when as a nation we professed to be Christians, we shed the blood of the martyrs. Thus when even such men as the great Sir Matthew Hale, one of the brightest Christian patterns in our country, were at the head of it, we condemned persons to death for witchcraft. But knowledge superior to that of those times, has taught us better things. By means of it we perceive, that persecution does not destroy, but that it propagates opinions, and that the belief of the existence of witchcraft is absurd.

These then appear to me to be the general advantages, or such as are inseparable from education when composed of the various branches of knowledge which have been described. I shall now endeavour to shew the peculiar advantages, which the Quakers would derive from it.

It will appear then, if we look back into the character of the Quakers, as described in this volume, that the world charges them, I mean the more affluent part of them, with having less learning, than others in a similar rank of life. But surely the education I propose would remove this intellectual defect.

The world again, as we have seen, has fixed another intellectual blemish upon them by the imputation of superstition. But how does superstition enter, but where there is a want of knowledge? Does not all history bear testimony, that in proportion as men have been more or less enlightened, they have been less or more liable to this charge? It is knowledge then, which must banish this frightful companion of the mind. Wherever individuals acknowledge, in a more extensive degree than others, the influence of the Divine Spirit in man, these, of all other people, will find the advantages of it. Knowledge leads to a solution of things, as they are connected with philosophy, or the theory of the human mind. It enables men to know their first and their second causes, so as to distinguish between causes and occasions. It fixes the nature of action and of thought; and, by referring effects to their causes, it often enables men to draw the line between the probability of fancy and inspiration. How many good men are there, who, adopting a similar creed with that of the Quakers on this subject, make themselves uneasy, by bringing down the Divine Being, promiscuously and without due discrimination, into the varied concerns of their lives? How many are there, who attribute to him that which is easily explained by the knowledge of common causes? Thus, for instance, there are appearances in nature, which a person of an uninformed mind, but who should adopt the doctrine of the influence of the Spirit, would place among signs, and wonders, and divine notices, which others, acquainted with the philosophy of nature, would almost instantly solve. Thus again there may be occasions, which persons, carrying the same doctrine to an undue extent, might interpret into warning or prophetic voices, but which a due exercise of the intellect, where such exercise has been properly encouraged, would easily explain. This reminds me of a singular occurrence: A friend of mine was lately walking in a beautiful vale. In approaching a slate-quarry he heard an explosion, and a mass of stone, which had been severed by gunpowder, fell near him as he walked along. He went immediately to the persons employed. He represented the impropriety of their conduct in not having given proper notice to such as were passing by, and concluded by declaring emphatically, that they themselves would be soon destroyed. It happened, but six weeks afterwards, that two of these men were blown to pieces. The words then of my friend were verified. Now I have no doubt that ignorant persons, in the habit of referring every thing promiscuously to the Divine interference, would consider my friend as a prophet, and his words as a divinely forewarning voice. But what did my friend mean? or where did he get his foresight on this occasion? The answer is, that my friend, being accustomed to the exercise of his rational faculties, concluded, that if the people in question were so careless with respect to those who should be passing by in such times of danger, they would by custom become careless with respect to themselves, and that ultimately some mischief would befal them. It is knowledge, then, acquired by a due exercise of the intellectual powers, and through the course of an enlightened education, which will give men just views of the causes and effects of things, and which, while it teaches them to discover and acknowledge the Divine Being in all his wondrous works, and properly to distinguish him in his providences, preserves them from the miseries of superstition.

The world again has fixed the moral blemish of the money-getting, spirit upon the Quaker character. But knowledge would step in here also as a considerable corrector of the evil. It would shew, that there were other objects besides money, which were worthy of pursuit. Nor would it point out only new objects, but it would make a scale of their comparative importance. It would fix intellectual attachments, next to religion, in the highest class. Thus money would sink in importance as a pursuit, or be valued only as it was the means of comfort to those who had it, or of communicating comfort to others. Knowledge also would be useful in taking off, to a certain degree, the corruptive effects of this spirit, for it would prevent it by the more liberal notions it would introduce, from leaving the whole of its dregs of pollution upon the mind.

The Quakers again, as we have seen, have been charged with a want of animation, from whence an unjust inference has been drawn of the coldness of their hearts. But knowledge would diminish this appearance. For, in the first place, it would enlarge the powers, and vary the topics of conversation. It would enliven the speaker. It would give him animation in discourse. Animation again would produce a greater appearance of energy, and energy of the warmth of life. And there are few people, whatever might be the outward cold appearance of the person with whom they conversed, whose prejudices would not die away, if they found a cheerful and an agreeable companion.

Another charge against the Quakers was obstinacy. This was shewn to be unjust. The trait, in this case, should rather have been put down as virtue. Knowledge, however, would even operate here as a partial remedy. For while the Quakers are esteemed deficient in literature, their opposition to the customs of the world, will always be characterized as folly. But if they were to bear in the minds of their countrymen a different estimation as to intellectual attainments, the trait might be spoken of under another name. For persons are not apt to impute obstinacy to the actions of those, however singular, whom they believe to have paid a due attention to the cultivation of their minds.

It is not necessary to bring to recollection the other traits that were mentioned, to see the operation of a superior education upon these. It must have already appeared, that, whatever may be the general advantages of learning, they would be more than usually valuable to the Quaker character.

CHAP. VI.

Arguments of those of the society examined, who may depreciate human knowledge—
This depreciation did not originate with the first Quakers—with Barclay—Penn—
Ellwood—but arose afterwards—Reputed disadvantages of a classical education—Its
heathen mythology and morality—Disadvantages of a philosophical one—Its
scepticism—General disadvantages of human learning—Inefficiency of all the arguments
advanced.

Having shewn the advantages, which generally accompany a superior
education, I shall exhibit the disadvantages which may be thought to attend
it, or I shall consider those arguments, which some persons of this society,
who have unfortunately depreciated human learning, though with the best
intentions, might use against it, if they were to see the contents of the
preceding chapter.

But, before I do this, I shall exonerate the first Quakers from the charge of
such a depreciation. These exhibited in their own persons the practicability
of the union of knowledge and virtue. While they were eminent for their
learning, they were distinguished for the piety of their lives. They were
indeed the friends of both. They did not patronize the one to the prejudice
and expulsion of the other.

[Footnote 53: George Fox was certainly an exception to this as a scholar.
He was also not friendly to classical learning on account of some of the
indelicate passages contained in the classical authors, which he and Farley
and Stubbs, took some pains to cite, but, if these had been removed, I
believe his objections would have ceased.]

Barclay, in his celebrated apology, no where condemns the propriety or
usefulness of human learning, or denies it to be promotive of the temporal
comforts of man. He says that the knowledge of Latin, Greek and Hebrew,
or of logic and philosophy, or of ethics, or of physics and metaphysics, is
not necessary. But not necessary for what? Mark his own meaning. Not
necessary to make a minister of the Gospel. But where does he say that
knowledge, which he himself possessed to such a considerable extent, was
not necessary, or that it did not contribute to the innocent pleasures of life?
What would have been the character of his own book, or what would have
been its comparative value and usefulness, if he had not been able to quote
so many authors to his purpose in their original texts, or to have detected
so many classical errors, or to have introduced such apposite history, or to
have drawn up his propositions with so much logical and mathematical

clearness and precision, or if he had not been among the first literary characters of his day?

William Penn was equally celebrated with Barclay as a scholar. His works afford abundant proof of his erudition, or of the high cultivation of his mind. Like the rest of his associates, he was no advocate for learning, as a qualification for a minister of the Gospel, but he was yet a friend to it, on the principle, that it enlarged the understanding, and that it added to the innocent pleasures of the mind. He entreated his wife, in the beautiful letter which he left her, before he embarked on his first voyage to America, "not to be sparing of expence in procuring learning for his children, for that by such parsimony all was lost that was saved." And he recommended also in the same letter the mathematical or philosophical education which I have described.

Thomas Ellwood, a celebrated writer among the early Quakers, and the friend of the great John Milton, was so sensible of the disadvantages arising from a want of knowledge, that he revived his learning, with great industry, even after he had become a Quaker. Let us hear the account which he gives of himself in his own Journal. "I mentioned before, says he, that, when I was a boy, I made some progress in learning, and that I lost it all again before I came to be a man. Nor was I slightly sensible of my last therein, till I came amongst the Quakers. But then I both saw my loss, and lamented it; and applied myself with the utmost diligence, at all leisure times to recover it. So false I found that charge to be, which in those times was east as a reproach upon the Quakers, that they despised and decried all human learning, because they denied it to be essentially necessary to a Gospel ministry, which was one of the controversies of those times."

"But though I toiled hard, and spared no pains to regain what I had once been master of, yet I found it a matter of so great difficulty, that I was ready to say, as the noble eunuch to Philip, in another case, how can I, unless I had some man to guide me?"

"This I had formerly complained of to my especial friend Isaac Pennington, but now more earnestly; which put him upon considering and contriving a means for my assistance."

"He had an intimate acquaintance with Dr. Paget, a physician of note in London, and he with John Milton, a gentleman of great note for learning, throughout the learned world, for the accurate pieces he had Written on various subjects and occasions."

"This person, having filled a public station in the former times, lived now a private and retired life in London; and, having wholly lost his sight, kept always a man to read to him, which usually was the son of some gentleman of his acquaintance, whom in kindness he took to improve in his learning."

"Thus by the mediation of my friend Isaac Pennington with Dr. Paget, and of Dr. Paget with John Milton, was I admitted to come to him; not as a servant to him (which at that time he needed not) nor to be in the house with him; but only to have the liberty of coming to his house at certain hours, when I would, and to read to him what books he should appoint me, which was all the favour I desired."

By means of this extract, made from the life of Thomas Ellwood, we come to three conclusions. First, that the early Quakers were generally men of eminent learning. Secondly, that they did not decry or depreciate human knowledge. And thirdly, that the calumny of such a depreciation by them arose from the controversy which they thought it right to maintain, in which they denied it to be necessary as a qualification for a Gospel minister.

This latter conclusion brings me round again to the point. And here I must observe, that, though this famous controversy occasioned the first Quakers to be unduly blamed on account of such a depreciation, yet it contributed to make some of their immediate successors, as I stated in a former volume, justly chargeable with it. But whether this was or was not the real cause, it is not material to the question. Many of the society, from came cause or other, did undoubtedly, in the age immediately succeeding that of their founders, begin to depreciate human knowledge, the effects of which, though gradually dissipating, have not been wholly done away at the present day. The disadvantages, therefore, of human learning, or the arguments which would be advanced against it by those who may undervalue it, I shall now consider.

These arguments may be divided into particular and general. On the former I shall first speak.

A classical education is considered to be objectionable, first, on account of the Heathen mythology that is necessarily connected with it. Its tendency, as it relates to fabulous occurrences, is thought to be unfavourable, as it may lead to a romantic propensity, and a turn for fiction. But surely the meaning of such occurrences cannot be well mistaken. If they are represented to our view in fable, they have had their foundation in truth. Many of them again are of such importance, that we could not wish to see them annihilated. Let us refer, for example, to the story of Deucalion and Pyrrha. Is it not one among the many outward confirmations of the truth of the history of Moses? Or do we not trace in it additional proofs of the deluge, and of the renewal of mankind?

Its tendency again, as it relates to the fabulous history of the Heathen gods, their number, their offices, and their character, is considered as degrading and exceptionable. I will concede this for a moment. But may it not, on the other hand, be rendered instructive and useful? May not the retention of such an history be accompanied with great moral advantages to our children? The emperor Theodosius commanded the idol temples to be destroyed. Instead of devoting them to the use of the Christians of those times, by which they might have been preserved to future generations, the most beautiful remains of antiquity were reduced to ruins. But would it not have been better, if Theodosius had brought good out of evil by retaining them? Would it not have been a high moral gratification to those who knew the fact, that temples, appropriated to the worship of idols, had been devoted to the service of the only true God? Would it not have been a matter of joy to these to have reflected upon the improving condition of mankind? And, while they looked up to these beautiful structures of art, might not the sight of them have contributed to the incitement of their virtue? If it be the tendency of the corrupt part of our nature to render innocent things vicious, it is, on the other hand, in the essence of our nature to render vicious things in process of time innocent, so that the very remnants of idolatry may be made subservient to our moral improvement. "If, as I observed in the first volume, we were to find an alter which had been sacred to Moloch, but which had been turned into a stepping-stone to help the aged and infirm upon their horses, why should we destroy it? Might it not be made useful to our morality, as for as it could be made to excite sorrow for the past and gratitude for the present?" And in the same manner the retention of the Heathen mythology might be made serviceable. Ought it not, whenever we contemplate it, to make us thankful, that we have not the dark and cheerless path of our ancestors to tread; that we have clearer light; that we have surer prospects; that we have a steadier ground of hope; and ought we not, on a contemplation of these superior advantages, brought to us by revelation, to be roused into the practice of a superior virtue.

Classical education again is considered as objectionable by the Quakers on account of the Heathen notions, which it may spread. Thus the highest reputation of man is placed in deeds of martial achievement, and a martial ardour is in consequence infused into youth, which it is difficult to suppress. That such notions and effect are produced, there can be no doubt; but how are we to avoid these whilst we are obliged to live in the world? The expulsion of the classics would not expel them. Our own newspapers, which are open to all, spread the same opinions, and are instrumental of course in producing the same excitements, but they do it in a much more objectionable way than the classical authors, that is, they do it with less delicacy, and with a more sanguinary applause. But where, as I observed before, shall we retire from such impressions? Does not the recruiting drum propagate them in all our towns? Do not the ringing of the bells, and the illuminations, which occasionally take place in the time of war, propagate them also? And do we not find these, both in war and in peace, the sentiments and impressions of the world? Our own notions then, our own writings, and our own customs, are more to be blamed in this respect, than the literary compositions of ancient times. But this, of all others, ought to be least an objection with the Quakers to such an education; because, to their honour, they have a constant counteraction of the effects of such sentiments and impressions in the principles of their own constitution, and which counteraction cannot cease, while, by the bearing of their testimony, they live in a continual protest against them.

The last objection to a classical education is, that the system of the Heathen morality is generally too deficient for those who are to be brought up as Christians. To this I answer, that it is quite as good as the system of the morality of the world. I could procure purer sentiments, and this generally from the Heathen authors usually called classical, than I can collect from many, even of the admired publications of our own times. The morality of the heathens is not so deficient as many have imagined. If their best opinions were duly selected and brought into one view, the only matter of surprise would be, how, with no other than the law written upon the heart, they had made such sublime discoveries. It was principally in their theology, where the law written upon the heart could not reach, that the ancients were deficient. They knew but little of the one true God. They did not know that he was a Spirit, and that he was to be worshiped in spirit and in truth. They were ignorant of his attributes. They had learnt nothing of the true origin, nature, and condition of man, or of the scheme of creation and redemption. These things were undoubtedly hidden from the eyes of the ancient philosophers. And it was in knowledge of this kind chiefly, that their deficiency was apparent. But how is this particular deficiency detrimental to youth, or how rather might it not be rendered useful to them in the way described? What a sublime contrast does knowledge, as exhibited by revelation, afford to the ignorance of those times, and what joy and gratitude ought we not to feel in the comparison? And this is the only use which can be made of their mythology? For when we send youth to the classical authors, we send them to learn the languages, and this through a medium where the morality is both useful and respectable, but we do not send them, living where the blessings of revelation are enjoyed, to be instructed in religion.

[Footnote 54: It must however be acknowledged, that, amidst beautiful sentiments, such as are indelicate are occasionally interspersed. But the quakers might remedy this objection by procuring a new edition of the purest classics only, in which particular passages might be omitted. They might also add new Latin notes, founded on Christian principles, where any ideas were found to be incorrect, and thus make Heathenism itself useful, as a literal teacher of a moral system. The world, I believe, would be obliged to the Quakers for such an edition, and it would soon obtain in most of the schools of the kingdom.]

The principal argument against a philosophical education, which is the next subject for consideration, is, that men, who cultivate such studies, require often more proofs of things than can always be had, and that, if these are wanting, they suspend their belief. And as this is true in philosophy, so it may be true in religion. Hence persons accustomed to such pursuits, are likely to become sceptics or infidels. To this I answer, that the general tendency of philosophy is favourable to religion. Its natural tendency is to give the mind grand and sublime ideas, and to produce in it a belief of the existence of one great cause, which is not visible among men. Thus, for example, I find that the planets perform a certain round! They perform it with a certain velocity. They do not wander at random, but they are kept to their orbits. I find the forces which act upon them for this purpose. I find, in short, that they are subject to certain laws. Now, if the planets were living agents, they might have prescribed these laws to themselves. But I know that this, when I believe them to consist of material substances, is impossible. If then, as material substances, they are subject to laws, such laws must have been given them. There must have been some lawgiver. In this manner then I am led to some other great, and powerful, and invisible Agent or Cause. And here it may be observed, that if philosophers were ever baffled in their attempts at discovery, or in their attempts after knowledge, as they frequently are, they would not, on this account, have any doubt with respect to the being of a God. If they had found, after repeated discoveries, that the ideas acquired from thence were repeatedly or progressively sublime, and that they led repeatedly or progressively to a belief of the existence of a superior Power, is it likely that they would all at once discard this belief, because there researches were unsuccessful? If they were to do this, they would do it against all the rules of philosophizing, and against the force of their own habits. I say, that analogical is a part of philosophical reasoning, and that they would rather argue, that, as such effects had been uniformly produced, so they would probably still be produced, if their researches were crowned with success. The tendency then of philosophical knowledge is far otherwise than has been supposed. And it makes highly in favour of the study of these sciences, that those who have cultivated them the most, such as Newton, and Boyle, and others, have been found among the ablest advocates for religion.

[Footnote 55: I by no means intend to say, that philosophy leads to the religion called Christianity, but that it does to Theism, which is the foundation of it.]

I come now, to the general arguments used by the Quakers against human learning, the first of which is, that they who possess it are too apt to reduce religion to reason, and to strip it of the influence of the Spirit. But this is contrary, as a general position, to all fact. We find no mention of this in history. The fathers of the church were the most eminent for learning in their own days, and these insisted upon the Influence of the Spirit in spiritual concerns, as one of the first articles of their faith. The reformers, who succeeded these, were men of extensive erudition also, and acknowledged the same great principle. And nine-tenths, I believe, of the Christians of the present, day, among whom we ought to reckon nine-tenths of the men of learning also, adopt a similar creed.

Another general argument is, that learning is apt to lead to conceit and pride, or to a presumed superiority of intellect, in consequence of which men raise themselves in their own estimation, and look down upon others as creatures of an inferior order of race. To this I may answer, that as prodigies are daily produced in nature, though they may be but as one to a hundred thousand when compared with the perfect things of their own kind, so such phenomena may occasionally make their appearance in the world. But as far as my own experience goes, I believe the true tendency of learning to be quite the reverse. I believe the most learned to be generally the most humble, and to be the most sensible of their own ignorance. Men, in the course of their studies, daily find something new. Every thing new shews them only their former ignorance, and how much there is yet to learn. The more they persevere, in their researches, the more they acknowledge the latter fact. The longer they live, the more they lament the shortness of life, during which, man with all his industry, can attain so little, and that, when he is but just beginning to know, he is cut off. They see, in short, their own nothingness, and, however they may be superior in their attainments, they are convinced that their knowledge is, after all, but a shadow; that it is but darkness; that it is but the absence of light; and that it no sooner begins to assume an appearance than it is gone.

The last general argument against learning is, that it does not lead to morality, or that learned men do not always exhibit an example of the best character. In answer to this I must observe, that the natural tendency of learning is to virtue. If learned men are not virtuous, I presume their conduct is an exception to the general effect of knowledge upon the mind. That there are, however, persons of such unnatural character, I must confess. But any deficiency in their example is not to be attributed to their learning. It is to be set down, on the other hand, to the morally defective education they have received. They have not been accustomed to wise restraints. More pains have been taken to give them knowledge, than to instruct them in religion. But where an education has been bestowed upon persons, in which their morals have been duly attended to, where has knowledge been found to be at variance, or rather where has it not been found to be in union, with virtue? Of this union the Quakers can trace some of the brightest examples in their own society. Where did knowledge, for instance, separate herself from religion in Barclay, or in Penn, or in Burroughs, or in Pennington, or in Ellwood, or in Arscott, or in Claridge, or in many others who might be named. And as this has been the case in the Quaker society, where a due care has been taken of morals, so it has been the case where a similar care has been manifested in the great society of the world.

"Piety has found
Friends In the friends of Science, and true pray'r
Has flow'd from lips wet with Castalian dews.
Such was thy wisdom, Newton, childlike sage!
Sagacious reader of the works of God,
And in his word sagacious. Such too thine,
Milton, whose genius had angelic wings,
And fed on manna. And such thine, in whom
Our British Themis gloried with just cause,
Immortal Hale! for deep discernment prais'd
And sound integrity not more, than fam'd
For sanctity of manners undefil'd." Cowper.

It appears then, if I have reasoned properly, that the arguments usually adduced against the acquisition of human knowledge are but of little weight. If I have reasoned falsely upon this subject, so have the early Quakers. As they were friends to virtue, so they were friends to science. If they have at any time put a low estimate upon the latter, it has been only as a qualification for a minister of the Gospel. Here they have made a stand. Here they have made a discrimination. But I believe it will no where be found, that they have denied, either that learning might contribute to the innocent pleasures of life, or that it might be made a subordinate and auxiliary instrument towards the promotion of virtue.

CHAP. VII.

Having now gone through all the subjects, which I had prescribed to myself at the beginning of this work, I purpose to close it. But as it should be the wish of every author to render his production useful, I shall add a few observations for this purpose. My remarks then, which will be thus conclusory, relate to two different sorts of persons. They will relate, first, to those who may have had thoughts of leaving the society, or, which is the same thing, who persist in a course of irregularities, knowing beforehand, and not regretting it, that they shall be eventually disowned. It will relate, secondly, to all other persons, or to those who may be called the world. To the former I shall confine my attention in this chapter.

I have often heard persons of great respectability, and these even in the higher circles of life, express a wish, that they had been brought up as Quakers. The steady and quiet deportment of the members of this society, the ease with which they appear to get through life, the simplicity and morality of their character, were the causes which produced the expression of such a wish. "But why then, I have observed, if you feel such a disposition as this wish indicates, do you not become Quakers?" "Because, it has been replied, we are too old to be singular. Dressing with sufficient simplicity ourselves, we see no good reason for adopting the dress of the society. It would be as foolish in us to change the colour and fashion of our clothing, as it would be criminal in the Quakers, with their notions, to come to the use of that which belongs to us. Endeavouring also to be chaste in our conversation, we cannot adopt their language. It would be as inconsistent in us to speak after the manner of the Quakers, as it would be inconsistent in them to leave their own language for ours. But we wish we had been born Quakers. And, if we had been born Quakers, we would never have deserted the society."

Perhaps they to whom I shall confine my remarks in this chapter, are not aware, that such sentiments as these are floating in the minds of many. They are not aware, that it is considered as one of the strongest things for those who have been born in the society, and been accustomed to its particularities, to leave it. And least of all are they aware of the worthless motives, which the world attributes to them for an intended separation from it.

There is, indeed, something seemingly irreconcileable in the thought of such a dereliction or change. To leave the society of a moral people, can it be a matter of any credit? To diminish the number of those who protest against war, and who have none of the guilt upon their heads of the sanguinary progress of human destruction which is going on in the world, is it desirable, or rather, ought it not to be a matter of regret? And to leave it at a time, when its difficulties are over, is it a proof of a wise and a prudent choice? If persons had ever had it in contemplation to leave the society in its most difficult and trying times, or in the days of its persecution, when only for the adoption of innocent singularities its members were insulted, and beaten, and bruised, and put in danger of their lives, it had been no matter of surprise: but to leave it, when all prejudices against them are gradually decreasing, when they are rising in respectability in the eyes of the government under which they live, and when, by the weight of their own usefulness and character, they are growing in the esteem of the world, is surely a matter of wonder, and for which it is difficult to account.

This brings me to the point in question, or to the examination of those arguments, which may at times have come into the heads of those who have had thoughts of ceasing to be members of this society.

In endeavouring to discover these, we can only suppose them to be actuated by one motive, for no other will be reasonable, namely, that they shall derive advantages from the change. Now all advantages are resolvable into two kinds, into such as are religious, and into such as are temporal. The first question then is, what advantages do they gain in the former case, or do they actually come into the possession of a better religion?

I am aware that to enter into this subject, though but briefly, is an odious task. But I shall abstain from all comparisons, by which I might offend any. If I were to be asked which, among the many systems of the Christian religion, I should prefer, I should say, that I see in all of them much to admire, but that no one of them, perhaps, does wholly, or in every part of it, please me; that is, there is no one, in which I do not see some little difficulty, which I cannot solve, though this is no impediment to my faith. But, if I were pressed more particularly upon this point, I should give the following answer. I should say, that I should prefer that, which, first of all, would solve the greatest number of difficulties, as far as scriptural texts were concerned, in conformity with the Divine attributes, which, secondly, would afford the most encouraging and consolatory creed, if it were equally well founded with any other; and which, thirdly, either by its own operation, or by the administration of it, would produce the post perfect Christian character. Let us then judge of the religion of the Quakers by this standard.

That there are difficulties with respect to texts of scripture, must be admitted; for if all men were to understand them alike, there would be but one profession of the Christian religion. One man endeavours to make his system comport wholly with human reason, and the consequence is, that texts constantly stare him in the face, which militate against it. Another discards reason, with a determination to abide literally by that, which is revealed, and the consequence is, that, in his literal interpretation of some passages, he leaves others wholly irreconcileable with his scheme. Now the religion, of the Quakers has been explained, and this extensively. In its doctrinal parts it is simple. It is spiritual. It unites often philosophy with revelation. It explains a great number of the difficult texts with clearness and consistency. That it explains all of them I will not aver. But these which it does explain, it explains in the strictest harmony with the love, goodness, justice, mercy, and wisdom of God.

As to the creed of the Quakers, we have seen its effects. We have seen it to be both encouraging and consolatory. We have seen it produce happiness in life, and courage in death. The doctrine of the possibility of human perfection, where it is believed, must be a perpetual stimulus to virtue, it must encourage hope and banish fear. But it may be said, that stimulative and consolatory as it may be, it wants one of the marks which I have insisted upon, namely, a sound foundation. But surely they, who deny it, will have as many scriptural texts against them as they who acknowledge it, and will they not be rendering their own spiritual situation perilous? But what do the Quakers mean by perfection? Not the perfection of God, to which there are no limits, as has been before explained, but that which arises to man from the possibility of keeping the divine commands. They mean that perfection, such as Noah, and Job, and Zacharias, and Elizabeth, attained, and which the Jewish rabbies distinguished by the name of Redemption, and which they conceived to be effected by the influence of the Holy Spirit, or that state of man in Christian morals, which, if he arrives at it, the Divine Being (outward redemption having taken place by the sacrifice of Christ) is pleased to accept as sufficient, or as the most pure state at which man, under the disadvantages of the frailty of his nature, can arrive. And is not this the practicable perfection, which Jesus himself taught in these words, "Be ye perfect, even as your Father, which is in heaven is perfect." Not that he supposed it possible, that any human being could be as perfect as the Divine Nature. But he proposed, by these expressions, the highest conceivable model of human excellence, of which our natures were capable, well knowing that the higher our aspirations the higher we should ascend, and the sooner we should reach that best state of humanity that was attainable. And here it is, that Christianity, as a rule of moral conduct, surpasses all others. Men, in general, look up to men for models. Thus Homer makes one of his heroes, when giving counsel to his son, say, "Always emulate the best." Thus also we should say to our children, if a person of extraordinary character were to live in our neighbourhood, "This is the pattern for your virture." But Jesus Christ says, aim at perfection beyond that which is human, alluding to the attributes of God, and thus you will attain a higher excellence than the study of any other model can produce.

With respect to the formation of man according to the model which Christianity prescribes, the system of the Quakers is no where to be excelled. No one, that we know of, is more powerful in the production of a subjugated mind and of a moral character. By this I mean, that there is none which is more universally powerful. It is the tendency of Christianity, whatever denomination it may assume, to produce these effects. But there is full as general an appearance of these among the Quakers, as in any other Christian profession.

It will appear then, that, if the three criterions, which have been specified, should be admitted to be those by which a judgment may be formed in the present case, they, who have had thoughts of leaving the society, will not be much better off by an exchange of their religion.

Let us see next, what would be the greater temporal advantages, which they would obtain. These may be summed up in two essential ingredients of happiness, in tranquillity of mind, in consequence of which we pass through the troubles of life in the most placid manner, and in a moderate pecuniary independence, in consequence of which we know none of the wants and hardships, but enjoy the reasonable comforts of it.

With respect to tranquillity of mind, we have shown this to be constitutional with the Quakers. It arises from their domestic enjoyments, from seldom placing their pleasures or their fortunes in the power of others, from freedom from the ambition and envyings of the world, from the regulation of the temper, from avoiding quarrels and lawsuits, and from other causes. And with respect to a moderate pecuniary independence, we have shewn not only that this is the general portion of the society, but that it is in the very nature of their habits to acquire it. Now these essential ingredients of happiness, or these temporal advantages, do not belong to the present Quakers only. They have always belonged to Quakers; and they will be perpetuated as an inheritance to their children, as long as Quakerism lasts. By this I mean to say, that if any Quakers, now living, could be sure that their descendants would keep to the wholesome regulations of the society for ten generations to come, they might have the comfort of believing, that tranquillity of mind would accompany them, as an effect of the laws and constitution belonging it, and that at any rate an easy pecuniary situation in life would be preserved to them. For if it be no difficult thing, with the natural habits of the society, to acquire an independence, it is much easier to preserve that which has been left them. But will they, who have had it in contemplation to leave the society, be able to say this for their children, when they adopt the world for their home? What certainty is there, that these will experience tranquillity, unless they are seen, quite as far as manhood, in the habits of religion? Will the cares of the world, its ambition, its thirst after honours, and its unbridled affections and passions, give them no uneasiness? And can the fortunes transmitted to them, subject as they will be to its destructive fashions and pleasures, be insured to them for even half of their times? How many have we seen, who have been in the prime of health in the morning, who have fallen before night in the duel? And how many have we seen in a state of affluence at night, who have been ruined by gaming in the morning?

But it is possible that they, who may have had thoughts of leaving the society; may picture to themselves another advantage, which I have not yet mentioned. It is possible, that there may be yet one which they may distinguish by such a name. They may possibly think it to be a gain to get rid of the restraint of the discipline of the society, and to enjoy the freedom of the world.

That the discipline is a restraint, I do not deny. But it must never be forgotten, that its object is moral good, and its effect the preservation of a moral character. But, come you, who complain of this heavy burden imposed upon you, and let us converse together for a moment, and let us see, if, when you relinquish it, you do not impose upon yourself a worse. Are you sure that, when you get rid of this discipline, you will not come under the discipline of fashion? And who is Fashion? Is she not of all mistresses the most imperious, and unreasonable, and cruel? You may be pleased with her for a while, but you will eventually feel her chains. With her iron whip, brandished over your head, she will issue out her commands, and you must obey them. She will drive you, without mercy, through all her corruptive customs, and through all her chameleon changes, and this against your judgment and against your will. Do you keep an equipage? You must alter the very shape of your carriage, if she prescribes it. Is the livery of your postilion plain? You must make it of as many colours as she dictates. If you yourself wear corbeau or raven colour to-day, you must change it, if she orders you, to that of puce, or the flea, to-morrow. But it is not only, in your equipage and your dress, that she will put you under her control. She will make you obedient to her in your address and manners.

She will force upon you rules for your intercourse with others. She will point out to you her amusements, and make you follow them. She will place you under her cruel laws of honour, from which she will disown you, if you swerve. Now I beseech you, tell me, which you think you would prefer, the discipline of the goddess Fashion, or that of the good old mistress, which you may have wished to leave? The one kindly points out to you, and invites and warns you to avoid, every dangerous precipice, that may be before you. The other is not satisfied, but with your destruction. She will force you, for a single word, uttered in a thoughtless moment, to run the hazard of your life, or to lose what she calls your character. The one, by preserving you in innocence, preserves you happy. The greater your obedience to her, the greater is your freedom; and it is the best species of freedom, because it is freedom from the pollutions of the world. The other awakens your conscience, and calls out its stings. The more obedient you are to her, the greater is your slavery, and it is the worst species of slavery, because it is often slavery to vice. In consequence of the freedom which the one bestows upon you, you are made capable of enjoying nature and its various beauties, and by the contemplation of these, of partaking of an endless feast. In consequence of the freedom which the one bestows upon you, you are made capable of enjoying nature, and its various beauties, and, by the contemplation, of these, of partaking of an endless feast. In consequence of the slavery to which the other reduces you, you are cramped as to such enjoyments. By accustoming you to be pleased with ridiculous and corruptive objects, and silly and corruptive changes, she confines your relish to worthless things. She palsies your vision, and she corrupts your taste. You see nature before you, and you can take no pleasure in it. Thus she unfits you for the most rational of the enjoyments of the world, in which you are designed to live.

CHAP. VIII.

Conclusory remarks, as they relate to those who compose the world at large—
Advantages, which these may derive from the contents of this work—from a view of many
of the customs—and of the principles explained in it—from seeing practically the
influence of these customs and principles in the production of character and happiness—
and from seeing the manner of their operation, or how they produce the effects described.

I shall now endeavour to make my conclusory remarks useful as they may relate to those who may be called the world.

To state the object, which I have in view, I shall observe at once, that men are divided in opinion as to the lawfulness, or expediency, or wholesomeness of many of the customs, fashions, and accomplishments of the world. We find some encouraging in their families, and this without any hesitation, and to an almost unlimited extent, those which many, on account of religious considerations, have expelled. We find others again endeavouring to steer a course between the opinions and practice of these. The same diversity of sentiment prevails also with respect to principles. The virtuous or moral are adopted by some. The political by others. That the political often obtain both in education and in subsequent life, there is no question. Thus, for example, a young man is thought by some to be more likely to make his way in the world with the address which fashionable accomplishments may give him, even if he be a little dissipated, than one of strict virtue with unpolished manners. Thus again in actions and transactions, policy is often preferred to express and open declarations of the truth. Others again are of opinion, that the general basis of principle should be virtue, but that a latitude may be, allowed for a seasonable policy. Thus an education is going on under Christian parents, as if Christianity had objects in view, which were totally opposite to each other.

It is in this point of view chiefly, that I can hope to be useful in this conclusory part of my work. We have seen in the course of it both customs and principles laid open and explained. We have seen the tendencies and bearings of these. We have seen them probed, and examined by a moral standard. We have seen their influence on character and happiness. We have seen the manner in which they act, or how these effects are produced. A revision therefore of these cannot but be useful, but more particularly to parents, as it may enable some of these, in conjunction with the knowledge they possess, to form probably a more correct system than they may have had it in contemplation to adopt, for the education of their youth.

The first advantage then, which those who compose the world at large may derive from the contents of this work, will be from a review of some of the customs which have been censured in it.

In looking into customs, the first that obtrudes itself upon our notice, is that of allowing to children those amusements, which, on account of the use of them, may be called gaming. A view is offered to us here, which is divested of all superstition. It is no where contended at random, in speaking against these, that their origin is objectionable. It is no where insisted upon, that there is evil in them considered abstractedly by themselves, or that they may not be used innocently, or that they may not be made the occasion of innocent mirth. The evil is candidly stated to arise from their abuse. The nature of this evil is unfolded. Thus the malevolent passions, such as anger, envy, hatred, revenge, and even avarice, are stirred up, where they should be particularly prevented, in the youthful breast. A spirit of gaming, which may be destructive of fortune, health, and morals, is engendered. A waste of time is occasioned, inasmuch as other pursuits might be followed, which would be equally amusing, but conducive to the improvement of the mind. The nature of the abuse is unfolded likewise. It consists of making games of chance productive of loss and gain. Thus they hold up speedy pecuniary acquisitions, and speedy repairs of misfortune. Thus they excite hope and fear, and give birth to pain and disappointment. The prevention also of the abuse, and that alone which can be effectual, is pointed out. This consists of a separation of emolument from chance, or of the adoption of the maxim, that no youth ought to be permitted to lay a wager, or to reap advantage from any doubtful event by a previous agreement on a moneyed stake. Now if the reader be not disposed to go the length which the Quakers do, by the abolition of such amusements, he will at least have had the advantage of seeing that there may be evil in them, and where it lies, and the extent (if he will only look at the historical instances cited) to which it may proceed, and its infallible prevention or its cure.

[Footnote 56: This argument is usually applied to grown up people, but may be applicable to youth, when we consider the ingenious inventions of modern times, such as maps of dissected geography, historical and other games, which, while they afford pleasure, promote improvement.]

The next subject which offers itself to our view, is music, and this comes before us in two forms, either as it is instrumental or vocal.

With respect to instrumental, it is no where insisted upon that its origin is evil, or that it is not productive of a natural delight, or that it does not soothe and tranquilize the passions, or that it may not be innocently used, or that it may not be made, under limitations, a cheerful companion in solitude. But it is urged against it, that it does not tend, like many other studies, to the improvement of the mind; that it affords no solid ground of comfort either in solitude or affliction; that it is a sensual gratification; and that sensual gratifications, if indulged in leisure hours, take up the time which should be devoted to those of a higher nature, that is, intellectual and moral pursuits. It is urged against it again, that, if abused, it is chargeable with a criminal waste of time, and a criminal impairing of health; that this abuse, in consequence of proficiency being insisted upon (without which it ceases to be delightful) is at the present day almost inseparable from its use; and that where the abuse of a thing, either in consequence of fashion, or its own seductive nature, or any other cause, is either necessarily or very generally connected with the use of it, watchfulness to avoid it is as much a duty in Christian morals, as it is a duty against the common dangers of life.

On vocal again we observe a proper distinction attempted. We find, that the singing is no more criminal than the reading of a song, being but another mode of expressing it, and that, the morality of it therefore will depend upon the words and sentiments it contains. If these are indelicate, or unchaste, or hold out false and corruptive ideas, as has been shewn to be the case with a variety of songs, then singing may from an innocent become a vicious amusement. But it has been observed, that youth seldom make any discrimination or selection with respect to songs, but that they pick up all that come in their way, whatever may be the impropriety of the words or sentiments, which they may contain.

Now then, whether we speak of instrumental or vocal music, if the reader should not be willing totally to discard this science as the Quakers do, he will at least have learnt some good from the observation which the work will have held out to him on this subject. He will see that evil may unquestionably be produced by the cultivation of it. He will see the absolute necessity of guarding his children against the learning of it to professional precision, as it is now unfortunately taught, to the detriment of their health, and of the acquisition of more important knowledge. He will see also the necessity of great vigilance with respect to the purity of the words and sentiments which may be connected with it.

The important subject, which is brought next before us, is that of the theatre. Here we are taught, that, though dramatic pieces had no censurable origin, the best of the ancient moralists condemned them. We are taught, that, even in the most favourable light in which we can view them, they have been thought objectionable, that is, that where they have pretended to teach morality, they have inculcated rather the refined virtue of heathenism, than the strict though mild morality of the Gospel; and where they have attempted to extirpate vice, they have done it rather by making it appear ridiculous, than by teaching men to avoid it as evil, or for the love of virtue. We are taught, that, as it is our duty to love our neighbour, and to be solicitous for his spiritual welfare, we ought not, under a system which requires simplicity and truth, to encourage him to be what he is not, or to personate a character which is not his own. We are taught that it is the general tendency of the diversions of the stage, by holding out false morals and prospects, to weaken the sinews of morality; by disqualifying for domestic enjoyments, to wean from a love of home; by accustoming to light thoughts and violent excitement of the passions, to unfit for the pleasures of religion. We are taught that diversions of this nature particularly fascinate, and that, if they fascinate, they suggest repetitions. And finally we are taught, that the early Christians on their conversion, though before this time they had followed them as among the desirable pleasures of their lives, relinquished them on the principles now explained.

The next subject, which comes to us in order, is dancing. This is handed down to us, under two appearances, either as it is simple, or as it is connected with preparations and accompaniments.

In viewing it in its simple state, it is no where contended, if it be encouraged on the principle of promoting such an harmonious carriage of the body, or use of the limbs, as maybe more promotive of health, that it is objectionable, though it is supposed that it is not necessary for such purposes, and that, without music and its other usual accompaniments, it would not be pleasant. Neither is it contended that a simple dance upon the green, if it were to arise suddenly and without its usual preparations, may not be innocent, or that if may not be classed with an innocent game at play, or with innocent exercise in the fields, though it is considered, that it would hardly be worthy of those of riper years, because they who are acknowledged to have come to the stature of men, are expected to abandon amusements for pursuits of usefulness, and particularly where they make any profession of the Christian name.

In viewing it with its preparations, and with its subsequent accompaniments, as usually displayed in the ball-room, we see it in a less favourable light. We see it productive, where it is habitually resorted to, of a frivolous levity, of vanity and pride, and of a littleness of mind and character. We see it also frequently becoming the occasion of the excitement of the malevolent passions, such as anger, envy, hatred, jealousy, malice, and revenge. We find it also frequently leading to indisposition. We find lastly, that, in consequence of the vexation of mind, which may arise from a variety of causes, but more particularly from disappointment and the ascendency of some of the passions that have been mentioned, more pleasure is generally perceived in the anticipation of these amusements, than in the actual taste or use of them.

[Footnote 57: Not only colds, head-aches, and a general lassitude, ore the result Of dancing in ball-rooms, but occasionally serious indisposition. I have known the death of two young persons attributed to it by the physicians who attended them in their illness.]

The subject of novels is presented next to our view. And here it has appeared, that no objection can be truly adduced against these on account of the fictitious nature of their contents. Novels also are not all of them promiscuously condemned. It is contended, however, from a variety of causes which were shewn, that they are very generally censurable. We are taught again, that the direct tendency of those which are censurable is to produce conceit and affectation, a romantic spirit, and a perverted morality among youth. We are taught again, that, on account of the peculiar construction of these, inasmuch as they have plot and character like dramatic compositions, they fascinate, and this to such a degree, that youth wait for no selection, but devour promiscuously all that come in their way. Hence the conclusion is, that the effects, alleged against novels, cannot but be generally produced. We are presented also with this fact, that, on account of the high seasoning and gross stimulants they contain, all other writings, however useful, become insipid. Hence the novel reader, by becoming indisposed to the perusal of more valuable books, excludes himself from the opportunity of moral improvement, and, if immoral sentiments are contracted, from the chance of any artificial corrective or cure.

The diversions of the field offer themselves next to our notice. We are taught, on the discussion which has arisen on this subject, that we are not permitted to take away the lives of animals wantonly but only as they may be useful for food, or as they may be dangerous to ourselves and to the other animals which may belong to us, and that a condition is annexed to the original grant or charter, by which permission was given to kill, which is never to be dispensed with, or, in other words, that we are to take away their lives as speedily as we can. Hence rights have sprung up on the part of animals, and duties on the part of men, any breach of which is the violation of a moral law. Hence the diversions of the field become often objectionable, because life is not thus taken away as speedily as it might otherwise have been, and because food or noxiousness is not often the object of the destruction of animals, but mere pleasure or sport. We are taught also to consider animals, not as mere machines, but as the creatures of God. We are taught also, that as they were designed to have their proper share of happiness during the time of their existence, any wanton interruption of this is an innovation of their rights as living beings. And we are taught finally, that the organic nature of men and animals being the same, as far as a feeling of pain is concerned, the sympathy which belongs to our nature, and the divine law of doing as we would be done by, which will hold as far as we can enter into the perceptions either of man or brutes, impose upon us the duty of anticipating their feelings, and of treating them in a corresponding or tender manner.

If we take a view of other customs, into which the Quakers have thought it right to introduce regulations with a view of keeping their members pure and innocent, we learn other lessons of usefulness. Thus, for example, the reader, if he does not choose to adopt their dress, may obtain desirable knowledge upon this subject. He will see that the two great objects of dress are decency and comfort. He will see, though Christianity prescribes neither colour nor shape for the clothing, that it is not indifferent about it. It enjoins simplicity and plainness, because, where men pay an undue attention to the exterior, they are in danger of injuring the dignity of their minds. It discards ornaments from the use of apparel, because these, by puffing up the creature, may be productive of vanity and pride. It forbids all unreasonable changes on the plea of conformity with fashion, because the following of fashion begets a worldly spirit, and because, in proportion as men indulge this spirit, they are found to follow the loose and changeable morality of the world, instead of the strict and steady morality of the Gospel.

On the subject of language, though the reader may be unwilling to adopt all the singularities of the Quakers, he may collect a lesson that may be useful to him in life. He may discover the necessity of abstaining from all expressions of flattery, because the use of these may be morally injurious to himself by abridging the independence of his mind, and by promoting superstition; while it may be injurious to others, by occasioning them to think more highly of themselves than they ought, and more degradingly of their fellow-creatures. He may discover also the necessity of adhering to the truth in all expressions, whether in his conversation or in his letters; that there is always a consistency in truth, and an inconsistency in falsehood; that as expressions accord with the essences, qualities, properties and characters of things, they are more or less proper; and that an attempt to adhere to the truth is productive of moral good, while a departure from it may lead into error, independently of its injury as a moral evil.

With respect to the address, or the complimentary gestures or ceremonies of the world, if he be not inclined to reject them totally as the Quakers do, he may find that there may be unquestionably evil in them, if they are to be adjudged by the purity of the Christian system. He may perceive, that there may be as much flattery and as great a violation of truth through the medium of the body, as through the medium of the tongue, and that the same mental degradation, or toss of dignified independence of mind, may insensibly follow.

On the subject of conversation and manners, he may learn the propriety of caution as to the use of idle words; of abstaining from scandal and detraction; of withholding his assent to customs when started, however fashionable, if immoral; of making himself useful by the dignity of the topic he introduces, and by the decorum with which he handles it; of never allowing his sprightliness to border upon folly, or his wit upon lewdness, but to clothe all his remarks in an innocent and a simple manner.

From the subject of customs connected with meals, such as that, for example, of saying grace, he may learn that this is a devotional act; that it is not to be said as a mere ceremony, by thanking the Supreme Being in so many words while the thoughts are roving on other subjects, but that it should be said with seriousness and feeling, and that it should never come as an oblation from the tongue, except it come also an oblation from the heart. And on that which relates to the drinking of toasts, he may see the moral necessity of an immediate extirpation of it. He may see that this custom has not one useful or laudable end in view; that it is a direct imitation of Pagans in the worst way in which we can follow them—their enjoyment of sensual pleasures; that it leads directly and almost inevitably to drunkenness, and of course to the degradation of the rational and moral character.

A second advantage, which they who compose the world may derive on this occasion, will be seen from a recapitulation of some of the principles which the work contains. The advantage in question will chiefly consist in this, that, whatever these principles may be, they may be said to be such as have been adopted by a moral people, and this after serious deliberation, and solely on a religious ground. It is of great importance from whence principles come recommended to our notice. If they come from the inconsiderate and worthless, they lose their value. If from the sober and religious, we receive them under the impression, that they may be promotive of our good. I shall give therefore a summary of these, as they may be collected from the work.

God has imparted to men a portion of his own Spirit, though he has given it to them indifferent degrees. Without this Spirit it would be impossible for them to discern spiritual things. Without this it would be impossible for them to know spiritually, even that the Scriptures were of divine authority, or spiritually to understand them. This Spirit performs its office of a teacher by internal monitions, and, if encouraged, even by the external objects of creation. It is also a primary and infallible guide. It is given to all without exception. It is given to all sufficiently. They who resist it, quench it, and this to their own condemnation. They who encourage it receive it more abundantly, and are in the way of salvation and redemption. This Spirit therefore becomes a Redeemer also. Redemption may he considered in two points of view, as it is either by outward or inward means, or as it relates to past sins or to sins to come. Jesus Christ effected redemption of the first kind, or that from past sins, while he was personally upon earth, by the sacrifice of himself. But it is this Spirit, or Christ within, as the Quakers call it, which effects the latter, or which preserves from future transgressions. It is this Spirit which leads, by means of its inward workings, to a new birth, and finally to the highest perfection of which our nature is capable. In this office of an inward Redeemer, it visits all, so that all may be saved, if they will attend to its saving operations, God being not willing that any should perish, but that all should inherit eternal life.

This Spirit also qualifies men for the ministry. It qualifies women also for this office as well as men. It dictates the true season for silence, and the true season for utterance, both in public and private worship.

Jesus Christ was man because he took flesh, and inhabited the body which had been prepared for him; but he was Divinity, because he was the Word.

A resurrection will be effected, but not of the body as it is. Rewards and punishments will follow, but guilt will not be imputed to men till they have actually committed sin.

Baptism and the Lord's Supper are essentials of the Christian religion. They are not, however, essentials as outward ordinances, but only as they are administered by the Holy Spirit.

Civil government is for the protection of virtue and for the removal of vice. Obedience should be paid to all its laws, where the conscience is not violated in doing it. To defraud it in any manner of its revenues, or to take up arms on any consideration against it, is unlawful. But if men cannot conscientiously submit to any one or more of its ordinances, they are not to temporize, but to obey Jesus Christ rather than their own governors in this particular case. They are, however, to be willing to submit to all the penalties which the latter may inflict upon them for so doing. And as no Christian ought to temporize in the case of any laws enjoined him by the government under which he lives, so neither ought he to do it in the case of any of the customs or fashions, which may be enjoined him by the world.

All civil oaths are forbidden in Christianity. The word of every Christian should be equivalent to his oath.

It is not lawful to return evil for evil, nor to shed the blood of man. All wars are forbidden.

It is more honourable, and more consistent with the genius and spirit of Christianity, and the practice of Jesus Christ and of his Apostles, and of the primitive Christians, that men should preach the Gospel freely, than that they should live by it, as by a profession or by a trade.

All men are brethren by creation. Christianity makes no difference in this respect between Jew and Gentile, Greek and Barbarian, bond and free. No geographical boundaries, nor colour of the skin or person, nor difference of religious sentiment, can dissolve this relationship between them.

All men are born equal with respect to privileges. But as they fall into different situations and ranks of life, they become distinguished. In Christianity, however, there is no respect of persons, or no distinction of them, but by their virtue. Nobility and riches can never confer worth, nor can poverty screen from a just appropriation of disgrace.

Man is a temple in which the Divinity may reside. He is therefore to be looked upon and treated with due respect. No Christian ought to lower his dignity, or to suffer him, if he can help it, to become the instrument of his own degradation.

Man is a being, for whose spiritual welfare every Christian should be solicitous, and a creature therefore worthy of all the pains that can be bestowed upon him for the preservation of his moral character.

The first object in the education of man should be the proper subjugation of his will.

No man ought to be persecuted or evil spoken of for a difference in religious opinion. Nor is detraction or slander allowable in any case.

Every religious community should consider the poor belonging to it as members of the same family, for whose wants and comforts it is a duty to provide. The education also of the children of these should be provided for.

It is enjoined us to live in peace with all men. All quarrels therefore are to be avoided between man and man. But if differences arise, they are to be adjusted by arbitration, and not, except it be otherwise impossible, by going to law, and never by violence.

If men offend against the laws, they should be prevented from doing injuries in future, but never by the punishment of the loss of life. The reformation of a criminal, which includes a prevention of a repetition of such injuries, is the great object to be regarded in the jurisprudence of Christians.

In political matters there is no safe reasoning but upon principle. No man is to do evil that good may come. The policy of the Gospel is never to be deserted, whatever may be the policy of the world.

Trade is an employment, by means of which we are permitted to gain a livelihood. But all trades are not lawful. Men are responsible, as Christians, for engaging in those which are immoral, or far continuing in those which they may carry on either to the moral detriment of themselves or of others. Abstinence from hazardous enterprises by the failure of which innocent persons might be injured, and honesty in dealing, and punctuality to words and engagements, are essentials in the prosecution of trade.

Having made observations on the customs, and brought to the view of the reader some of the prominent principles of the Quakers, a third advantage will arise from knowing the kind of character, which these in conjunction will produce.

On this subject we might be permitted our conjectures. We might insist upon the nature and immediate tendencies of these customs and principles, and we might draw our conclusions from thence, or we might state how they were likely to operate, so as probably not to be far from the truth. But we are spared both the trouble of such a task, and are relieved from the fear of having the accuracy of our conclusions doubted. The Quaker character has been made up from the acknowledgments of others. It has been shewn that they are a moral people; that they are sober, and inoffensive, and quiet; that they are benevolent to man in his religious and temporal capacity; that they are kind or tender-hearted to animals; that they do not make sacrifices of their consciences to others; that in political affairs they reason upon principle; that they are punctual to their words and engagements; and that they have independence of mind, and courage. Their character, as it is defective, has been explained also. It has been probed, and tried by a proper touchstone. Appearances have been separated from realities. The result has been, that a deficiency in literature and science, and that superstition, and that an undue eagerness after money, has been fixed upon a portion of them. The two former, however, it is to be recollected, are only intellectually defective traits, and maybe remedied by knowledge. The latter, it is to be presumed, belongs rather to individuals than to the society at large. But whatever drawbacks may be made from the perfect by the imperfect qualities that have been stated, there is a great preponderancy on the side of virtue. And where, when we consider the evil propensities of our nature, and the difficulty of keeping these in due order, are we to took for a fairer character? That men, as individuals, may be more perfect, both in and out of the society, is not to be denied. But where shall we find them purer as a body? and where shall we find a faulty character, where the remedy is more easily at hand?

The next advantage will be in seeing the manner of the operation of these customs and principles, or how they act. To go over the whole character of the Quakers with this view would be both tedious and unnecessary. I shall therefore only select one or two parts of it for my purpose. And first, how do these customs and principles produce benevolence? I reply thus: The Quakers, in consequence of their prohibitions against all public amusements, have never seen man in the capacity of a hired buffoon or mimic, or as a purchasable plaything. Hence they have never viewed him in a low and degrading light. In consequence of their tenet on war, they have never viewed him as an enemy. In consequence of their disciplinary principles, they have viewed him as an equal. Hence it appears, that they have no prejudices against him from causes which often weigh with others, either on account of rank, or station, or many of the customs of the world. Now I conceive, that the dereliction of prejudice against man is as necessary, as a first measure, to the production of benevolence towards him, as the dereliction of vice towards the production of virtue. We see then their minds free from bias on this subject. But what is there on the other side to operate actively towards the promotion of this trait? They view man, in the first place, as the temple in which the Divinity may reside. This procures him respect. Secondly, as a being for whose spiritual welfare they ought to be solicitous. This produces a concern for him. And thirdly, as a brother. This produces relationship. We see then the ground cleared. We see all noxious weeds extirpated. We see good seed sown in their places; that is, we see prejudices removed from the heart, and we see the ideas of respect, concern, and relationship implanted in it. Now it is impossible that these ideas, under these circumstances, should not as naturally and immediately produce a general benevolence to man, as common seeds, when all obstructive weeds are removed, should produce their corresponding saplings or flowers.

How again are these customs and principles of the Quakers promotive of independence of mind? I answer thus: There is a natural independence of mind in man, but it is often broken and weakened. Some men injure it by the solicitation and acceptance of honours, and pensions, and places; others by flattery and falsehood; others by customs of obeisance; others by their obedience to fashion. But the independence of mind of the Quakers is not stunted in its growth by the chiding blasts of such circumstances and habits. It is invigorated, on the other hand, by their own laws. No servility is allowed either in word or gesture. Neither that which is written, nor that which is uttered, is to please the vanity of the persons addressed, or to imply services never intended to be performed. The knee is not to be bent to any one. It is strengthened again and made to shoot by their own maxims. Is it possible to be in the habit of viewing all men as equal in privileges, and no one as superior to another but by his virtue, and not to feel a disposition that must support it? Can the maxim of never doing evil that good may come, when called into exercise, do otherwise than cherish it? And can reasoning upon principle have any other effect than that of being promotive of its growth?

These then are the ways in which these customs and principles operate. Now the advantage to be derived from seeing this manner of their operation, consists in this: First, that we know to a certainty, that they act towards the production of virtue. Knowing again what these customs and principles are, we know those which we are bound to cherish. We find also, that there are various springs which act upon the moral constitution for the formation of character. We find some of these great and powerful, and others inferior. This consideration should teach us not to despise even those which are the least, if they have but a tendency to promote our purity. For if the effect of any of them be only small, a number of effects of little causes or springs, when added together, may be as considerable as a large one. Of these again we observe, that some are to be round where many would hardly have expected them. This consideration should make us careful to look into all our customs and principles, that we may not overlook any one which we may retain for our moral good. And as we learn the lesson of becoming vigilant to discover every good spring, and not to neglect the least of these, however subtle its operation, so we learn the necessity of vigilance to detect every spring or cause, and this even the least, whether in our customs or our principles, if it should in its tendency be promotive of vice.

And in the same manner we may argue with respect to other productions of these customs and principles of the Quakers. As we have seen the latter lead to character, so we have seen them lead to happiness. The manner of their operation to this end has been also equally discernible. As we value them because they produce the one, so we should value them because they produce the other. We have seen also which of them to value. And we should be studious to cherish the very least of these, as we should be careful to discard the least of those which are productive of real and merited unhappiness to the mind.

And now, having expended my observations on the tendencies of the customs and principles of the Quakers, I shall conclude by expressing a wish, that the work which I have written may be useful. I have a wish, that it may be useful to those who may be called the world, by giving them an insight into many excellent institutions, of which they were before ignorant, but which may be worthy of their support and their patronage. I have a wish also, that it may be useful to the Quakers themselves, first, by letting them see how their own character may be yet improved; and secondly, by preserving them, in some measure, both from unbecoming remarks, and from harsh usage, on the part of their fellow-citizens of a different denomination from themselves. For surely when it is known, as I hope it is by this time, that they have moral and religious grounds for their particularities, we shall no longer hear their scruples branded with the name of follies and obstinacies, or see magistrates treating them with a needless severity, but giving them, on the other hand, all the indulgences they can, consistently with the execution of the laws. In proportion as this utility is produced, my design will be answered in the production of the work, and I shall receive pleasure in having written it. And this pleasure will be subject only to one drawback, which will unavoidably arise in the present case; for I cannot but regret that I have not had more time to bestow upon it, or that some other person has not appeared, who possessing an equal knowledge of the Quakers with myself, but better qualified in other respects, might have employed his talents more to the advantage of the subjects upon which I have treated in these volumes.

[Footnote 58: Some magistrates, much to their honour, treat them with tenderness; and no people are more forward than the Quakers in acknowledging any attention that may be shewn them, but particularly where their religious scruples may be concerned.]

END OF THE THIRD VOLUME